P9-DFJ-153

Better Homes and Gardens®

Wreaths and Other Nature Crafts

Better Homes and Gardens®

Wreaths *and* Other Nature Crafts

Better Homes and Gardens® Books
Des Moines, Iowa

Better Homes and Gardens® Books is an imprint of Meredith® Books

President, Book Group: Joseph J. Ward

Vice President, Editorial Director: Elizabeth P. Rice

Executive Editor: Maryanne Bannon

Senior Editor: Carol Spier

Editor: Ron Harris

Creative Editorial Coordinator: Alexandra Hay Eames

Production Manager: Bill Rose

Photographs: Bruce McCandless

Illustrations: Laura Hartman Maestro

Editorial production and design by Barclay House Publishing

Director: Barbara Machtiger

Designer: Robert E. Kiley

Copy Editor: Sydne Matus

Copyright © 1995 by Meredith Corporation. All rights reserved.
Distributed by Meredith Corporation, Des Moines, Iowa.

Brief quotations may be used in critical articles and reviews. For any other reproduction of this book, however, including electronic, mechanical, photocopying, recording, or other means, written permission must be obtained from the publisher.

ISBN: 0-696-01957-4

Library of Congress Catalog Card Number: 93-080857

Printed in the United States of America

10 9 8 7 6 5 4 3 2 1

All of us at Better Homes and Gardens® Books are dedicated to offering you, our customer, the best books we can create. We are particularly concerned that all of our instructions for making projects are clear and accurate. Please address your correspondence to Customer Service, Meredith Press, 150 East 52nd Street, New York, NY 10022.

If you would like to order additional copies of any of our books, call 1-800-678-8091 or check with your local bookstore.

Preface

Better Homes and Gardens® *Wreaths and Other Nature Crafts* is for all who love nature, enjoy the outdoors, and are happiest working with their hands. The six chapters of craft projects use simple techniques and rely on nature's own complex textures, colors, and shapes for their unusual beauty. You need not be skilled or long on patience to create interesting and decorative results. Each project includes a full-page color photo, a list of Nature's Materials and of Supplies and Tools, plus easy-to-follow, step-by-step directions with diagrams where necessary to explain procedures more clearly.

Five of the six project chapters highlight a particular natural environment, from the garden to the seashore, and the projects are made from the materials found there. Most—such as leaves, branches, and grasses—are within easy access, even in urban areas. The more exotic ingredients (for example, bird feathers and self-hardening clay) can be ordered by mail (the resource list in back tells you where) or purchased in a craft shop. The sixth hands-on chapter features a potpourri of decorations you can make to dress your home for holidays or with the changing seasons. The last chapter, "Nature Crafts Basics," supplies information and instructions on the fundamental techniques used repeatedly throughout the book and presents an overview of the commonplace tools you'll need for making the projects. The resource list at the back of the book includes the names and addresses of suppliers of materials.

Much of the pleasure of these nature craft projects is in making them, but even more comes from looking, searching, and seeing nature in a new way.

Acknowledgments

The expertise, talent, and ideas of craft designers form the substance of this book. When given merely the suggestion of natural materials—leaves, bark, stones, or flowers—they returned with lists of projects, enough for several books. Their enthusiasm and fascination with the variety of shapes, textures, and colors led to unusual results. An ordinary leaf became the mast of a boat, a slice of orange became stained glass, a glittery stone found beside a stream became a jeweled pendant, and birdseed turned into siding for artistic birdhouses.

We thank the following artists and designers for their contributions and, especially, for their individual points of view: Wilanna Bristow, for the innovative use of pumpkin and squash seeds in embroidery; Diana Conklin of Everlastings by Diana, for lush arrangements of dried flowers and grasses; Ginger Hansen Shafer, for unraveling the mysteries of papermaking, straw ornaments, Easter eggs, and working with pressed flowers; Jackie Smyth, for her charming woodland dolls and sunprints; Brent Pallas, an urban woodsman, for his walking sticks, twig furniture, and the patinated wreath; Yvonne Beecher, for the clay and stone jewelry, crocheted raffia baskets, herb garden markers, and starfish ornaments; Mimi Shimmin, for the birdseed birdhouses, lavender sachets, herb wreath, and Christmas decorations; Evelyn Fell, with her partners Leslie Grayson and Barbie Smith of Remember When Flowers, for the seashell topiaries, unusual wreaths, and holiday decorations; and Callie Greene, for her naturalist's view on masks and tiny seashell boxes.

All these people contributed far more than the projects mentioned. Their ability, insight, and commonsense approach to working with natural materials make nature crafts accessible and pleasurable. Many thanks are due to Florence Fink, Virginia Jerman, and David and Anne Cripps for offering their homes as locations for photography. Thank you to the manufacturers who provided tools and materials and, in many instances, mail-order availability for their products. Their names and addresses are listed in Resources on page 205.

Many new friends have been made and ideas exchanged across the crafts network, a congenial world where designers, suppliers, and manufacturers all seem to enjoy their work and are eager to share it with you, the reader.

Contents

Introduction	**9**
Gardens	**10**
Teacup Tussie-mussies	12
Floral Picture Frame	14
Ivy Topiary Wreaths and Tree	15
Pressed-Flower Lampshade	18
Herb Wreath	20
Lavender Sachets	22
Flower-Trimmed Hat	23
Gourd Birdhouse	24
Dried Citrus Wreath	26
Pressed-Flower Candles and Floral Candle Wreath	28
Kitchen Topiaries	30
Eggshell Mosaic Frame	32
Eggshell Vases	34
Citrus Box and Pouch	35
Seed-Covered Birdhouses	37
Seed Embroidery	41
Handmade Note Paper, Gift Boxes, and Bookmark	45
Woodlands	**48**
Maple Leaf Roses	50
Oak Leaf Wreath	52
Stenciled Leaf Tray	54
Stenciled Leaf Napkin and Gilded Acorn Napkin Ring	55
Bark Berry Basket	57
Bark Wall Pocket	59
Branch Table Lamp	60
Twig Torchères	63
Branch Birdbath	64
Birch Bark Box	67
Birch Bark Wreath	69
Wood Nymph Masks	70
Miniature Twig Furniture	72
Spring and Fall Dolls	78
Thickets and Grasslands	**82**
Wild Grass Sheaf	84
Bittersweet Door Garland	86
Bittersweet Basket	88
Twig Swirl Wreath	90
Twig Planter	92
Feather Mask	93
Crocheted Raffia Baskets	96
Bamboo Easels	99
Door Spray	102
Walking Sticks	104
Twig Boats	106
Streams and Marshes	**108**
Clay Bead Jewelry	110
Moss-Covered Flowerpot	114
Moss Wreath	116
Driftwood-and-Sand Frame	117
Southwest Sand Garden	119
Pressed Ferns	120

Stone Herb Markers   122

Sunprint Sachets   124

Crystal Jewelry   127

The Seashore   130

Scallop Shell Boxes   132

Shell-Covered Box   134

Dresser Set   136

Shell Wreaths   138

Shell Lamp Finials   140

Seashell Topiaries   142

Tablecloth Hold-downs   144

Raffia-and-Shell Tieback   146

Shell Curtain Holdback   148

Shell-and-Starfish Curtain
    Ring Covers   149

Starfish Curtain Pole Finial   152

Seasonal Decorations   154

Gilded Magnolia Garland
    and Sprays   156

Gilded Gift Wrap   160

Handmade Valentines   162

Patinated Wreath   164

Patinated Eggs   166

Twig Easter Basket   168

Easter Egg Bunny   170

Leaf-Resist, Dyed,
    and Gilded Eggs   171

Cornucopia Centerpiece   173

Pinecone Flower Vase   175

Spiral Topiary   176

Golden Grapevine Wreath   178

Pumpkin Centerpiece   179

Mantel Garland   181

Braided-Wheat Ornaments   184

Christmas Starfish Ornaments   188

Nature Crafts Basics   192

Tools and Supplies   194

Drying Plants, Leaves, Flowers,
    Fruits, and Vegetables   195

Preserving Plants with Glycerin   197

Pressing Flowers and Leaves   198

Cleaning Shells and Other
    Seashore Materials   198

Basic Dyes from Plant Material   199

Grapevine Wreath   200

Handmade Paper   200

Resources   205

Index   207

Introduction

Nature provides the materials for the craft projects in this book. Whether you live in the city or the country, the leaves, branches, grasses, stones, and shells will be familiar. Regardless of the setting, the search for your materials will be an important part of the pleasure of creating these projects. By looking and seeing, evaluating the possibilities nature offers, you will become a better observer and much more aware of the beauty around you. For example, if you are a seasoned hiker at home in the wilderness, you will discover fantastic miniature worlds along the side of a stream when searching for the perfect piece of moss. You may stop to notice the many colors and textures of the grasses at the side of the path or the shapes of the pinecones above your head. Nature has many surprises: hidden under leaves, inside an old stump, or just creeping out from under your shoe.

Psychologists now feel that getting out into the countryside, away from everyday cares, can bring a new perspective. Many of us have become so stressed that we have become insensitive to our surroundings, so out of touch that we no longer care about our role in nature, our effect on it, or its effect on us. Nature is exceedingly generous, offering a change of pace in many ways: a chance to exercise in fresh air, to feel changes in temperature and humidity, and to hear natural sounds—the gentle hum of insects, the rustle of leaves blown by the wind, and the chatter of birds. Even if you live on a farm, its daily routine can overwhelm your thoughts. A casual walk to a thicket to collect grapevines may provide the break and the inspiration you need.

We are all part of nature, and we share the benefits and consequences of nature's condition. By becoming better acquainted with and more aware of what is happening to our natural world, we can promote its health and productivity. This means respecting nature. When we venture into the woods looking for bark for a project, we should take pieces from fallen logs, not cut into a living tree. Girdling a tree (cutting the bark all the way around the trunk) will cut its lifeline to its roots and kill it. Native Americans, who have lived in harmony with nature for thousands of years, learned to take only small portions of each resource, so that nature could replace what was taken. When they cut branches of a plant, they would take only one or two, leaving the rest to grow. We can do the same (for example, by collecting only empty shells for shell projects or by gathering only a few small clumps of moss from different areas, so the main plant will grow back).

Respect for property owners is also important. Always ask permission to gather lichen or cut vines on private property and respect the rules of public parks and nature preserves. Areas with trail systems advise staying on the trails to prevent damage to fragile plants and ecosystems. Often casual berry picking or the gathering of a few leaves is permitted when commercial harvesting is not. Get to know your local parks and preserves and the people assigned to their conservation and care.

The designers of the projects in this book were most enthusiastic. They have learned to see nature from a different point of view and to turn their unusual outlooks into original creations. Their ability to look at a leaf and see a mask or to examine a bit of Spanish moss and visualize it as doll's hair makes each project unusual and fun. We applaud their vision, wit, and ability to share their ideas with the rest of us. The people you meet while gathering your materials— whether the craft shop owner or the next-door neighbor—may also become collaborators or sources for materials. Ideas can come from just about anywhere.

Gardens

For many, nature and her abundant materials are just outside the door. Frontyard borders and backyard plots provide a wealth of leaves, branches, blossoms, and seeds—the main ingredients in many of the following garden craft projects. Vegetables and flowers provide not only the colors for natural dyes to tint both eggshells and handmade paper, but also the raw materials for pressing and drying. In rural areas the garden may also be home to chickens and ducks who produce eggs in a gentle spectrum of color for eggshell mosaics. Lofty sunflowers supply the seeds for indoor birdhouses, and pumpkins furnish the ornaments for fanciful seed embroidery. Urban dwellers will find nature's offerings in a window herb planter or in colorful profusion at the local florist. Leaves from indoor plants can be pressed as easily as those that grow outdoors. Farmer's markets and grocery stores are handy resources for plant varieties not found in your own area. Remember too that gardeners, wherever they live, are masters of the art of barter, trading plants and cuttings from their crowded beds and sharing the harvest when their gardens are prolific—especially if you ask.

Teacup Tussie-mussies

Victorians gave tussie-mussies (miniature bouquets) as tokens of affection and as a way of silently expressing themselves, although assigning hidden meanings to flowers did not originate or end with them. A gift of roses delivered with a calling card, for example, declares love the world over, but did you know that blue violets profess faithfulness, that angelica indicates inspiration, and that yarrow represents solace? (See the box below for other flowers and their meanings.) The tussie-mussies here are truly of today despite their nineteenth-century teacup and cream pitcher containers. The flowers shown are dried and include a poppy pod (the red poppy suggests consolation), larkspur (for levity), and roses (for love). For instructions and information on drying flowers see Nature Crafts Basics.

SIZE

Tussie-mussies shown are 4½" in diameter

NATURE'S MATERIALS

For one tussie-mussie

Dried flowers: 6 stalks of wheat; 3 or 4 purple nigella; 2 stems of each color larkspur in pink, blue, and white; 2 red roses; 1 small red cockscomb; 1 small cluster of hydrangea; 1 poppy pod; 1 head of yellow yarrow

SUPPLIES AND TOOLS

Container of choice

Floral foam to fit container

Utility knife   Scissors

Hot-glue gun and glue stick

DIRECTIONS

1. With the knife cut a 1"-thick block of floral foam to fit snugly into the container.

2. With scissors, trim the stems of the wheat stalks, leaving enough of a stem to insert into the foam. Insert the stalks into the center of the foam, arranging them in a tight cluster.

3. Working from the center out toward the rim of the cup, continue adding flowers in clusters, positioning shorter flowers and stems near the edges so the arrangement slopes to the rim. Some flowers may need a dot of hot glue to hold them in place. Fill in any gaps with larkspur to cover the foam base.

❧ The Language of Flowers ❧

Bluebell: *constancy; kindness*
Buttercup: *cheerfulness*
Carnation: *fascination*
Columbine: *folly*
Crocus: *abuse not*
Daffodil: *regard*
Daisy: *innocence*
Forget-me-not: *remembrance; don't forget me*

Hollyhock: *fruitfulness*
Honeysuckle: *bond of love*
Imperial lily: *majesty*
Ivy: *friendship*
Lavender: *distrust*
Lilac, purple: *blossoming love*
Lily of the valley: *return of happiness*
Lobelia: *malevolence*

Mountain laurel: *glory*
Pansy: *thoughts; I'm thinking of you*
Pennyroyal: *flee away*
Peony: *bashfulness*
Rhododendron: *danger*
Sage: *esteem*
Sweet William: *finesse*
Tulip, red: *declaration of love*

Floral Picture Frame

Dried flowers can add meaning to the frame for a sentimental photograph, such as the one here of a young girl in her Queen of Hearts costume covered with lacy hearts and flowers. Coordinate the colors of the flowers with the subject matter of the photo: bright colors for a birthday snapshot or soft whites and pastels for a wedding portrait. For instructions and information on drying flowers see Nature Crafts Basics.

SIZE

Frame shown is 7½" × 9½"

NATURE'S MATERIALS

Dried flowers: wheat, roses, hydrangea, pepper berries or any berry, pod, or nut

SUPPLIES AND TOOLS

Wood picture frame with glass and easel back

Photo mat or colored paper backing to coordinate with flowers, cut to fit frame

Photograph of choice

Spray paint in white or color of choice

Scissors

Hot-glue gun and glue stick

Newspaper

DIRECTIONS

1. Remove the back and the glass from the picture frame. Lay the frame on newspaper that is spread in a well-ventilated area. Following the manufacturer's directions, spray several light coats of paint for the desired coverage. An uneven coat with the original color showing through in some areas will give an antique effect. Let dry.

2. Using scissors, cut the tips off the wheat stalks, leaving a 2" stem. Hot-glue 2 clusters of wheat at right angles to each other onto diagonally opposite corners of the frame. Glue the roses to the bottom corner of the frame and the pepper berries to the top. Fill in with hydrangea blossoms.

3. Mount the photograph on the mat or colored paper backing, cover with the glass, and carefully insert into the back of the frame without crushing the flowers on the front. Replace the easel back. If you prefer, you can insert the matted photograph and the glass after you paint the frame but before you decorate it.

Ivy Topiary Wreaths and Tree

Topiary is the art of training and clipping living plants (usually boxwood, hemlock, or privet hedging) into ornamental shapes, as was done with the small-leafed English ivies shown here. Supported by a bent coat hanger or heavy wire, the young tendrils can be trained in any direction. When the topiary is well established, occasional trimming will keep it in shape. Two-inch-long cuttings from the larger triangular plant were rooted in water for a couple of weeks and used to make the two wreaths, which are about eight months old and still filling out. Wire topiary forms are available in craft and floral supply shops, or you can make your own in any shape.

SIZES

As shown:

Tree is 17" high, including pot

Wreaths are 11" high, including pots

NATURE'S MATERIALS

For one topiary

Small-leafed ivy plants, 3 plants per pot or 4–5 rooted cuttings

Potting soil

Several pebbles for the bottom of the pot

SUPPLIES AND TOOLS

Clay flowerpot, 6" in diameter or in size desired

Coat hangers (1 for each wreath; 2 for tree shape) or heavy-gauge floral wire

Fine-gauge floral wire

Green floral tape

Long-nosed pliers

Wire cutters

Pruning shears or scissors

Gardening gloves

DIRECTIONS

1. Wearing gloves to protect your hands, straighten the hook of the coat hanger with long-nosed pliers. This will be the stem of the topiary that is stuck into the potting soil. For the tree-shaped form, use 2 coat hangers for added support. Pull the wire of each hanger up, shape it into a triangle, and tape the 2 forms together with floral tape as illustrated. Start at the stem and work on the diagonal, wrapping the tape up and around the forms. For the wreath shape use 1 coat hanger. Pull it up and bend it into a large circle. Then, by twisting it in a figure-eight pattern, make 2 circles half the original size. Bend the circles in toward each other and wrap them together with floral tape as illustrated. Leave the stems bare. Don't worry if your shapes are not exact; the ivy will obscure the wire.

2. Place several pebbles in the bottom of the flowerpot for drainage. Fill the pot half full with potting soil. Insert the stem of the wire form into the soil. Make sure the bottom of the triangle or circle is level with the rim of the pot. Pat down the soil firmly around the stem. Add more soil and pack it to make the form stand up. Water the soil and let drain.

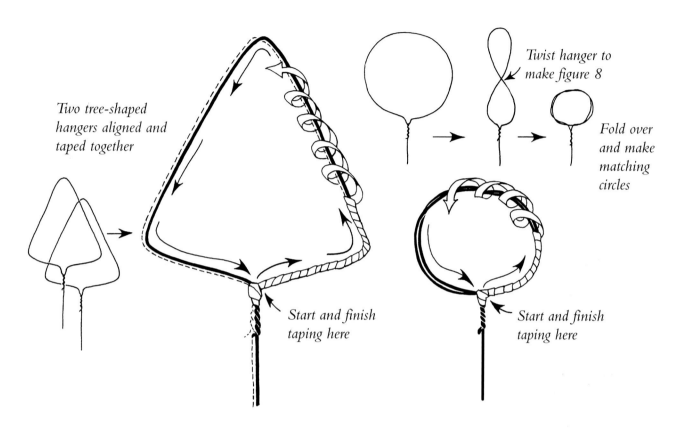

Two tree-shaped hangers aligned and taped together

Start and finish taping here

Twist hanger to make figure 8

Fold over and make matching circles

Start and finish taping here

Tree-Shaped Topiary Form   **Wreath-Shaped Topiary Form**

3. Plant the small ivy plants or rooted cut-tings at the base of the wire form. Twine the branches of ivy around the form and loosely wrap with fine floral wire to secure them to the form. As they grow you will be able to wrap the longer tendrils around and through existing ivy without using wire.

4. Water the plants well and feed them occasionally with liquid fertilizer. Continue to tuck new tendrils in and around the form as they grow. When the plant has covered the entire form, cut back the longer tendrils to encourage thicker growth. Save the cuttings for more topiaries.

Pressed-Flower Lampshade

Découpage, French for "cutting up," is an art form that usually involves pasting printed paper cutouts—often of flowers, animals, and birds—to a surface and then coating them with a protective varnish. Here the cutouts are the real thing—pressed pansy blossoms and sage leaves—gracing a ready-made cloth-covered lampshade. Several finishing coats of découpage medium create a long-lasting surface that can be wiped clean with a damp cloth. For instructions and information on pressing flowers and leaves see Nature Crafts Basics.

SIZE

For lamp of choice

NATURE'S MATERIALS

Assorted pressed flowers, leaves, and herbs

SUPPLIES AND TOOLS

Paper or cloth-covered lampshade

Découpage medium (a sealer, glue, and finish, such as Mod-Podge™)

Paintbrush

Tweezers

DIRECTIONS

1. Brush a thin coat of découpage medium onto the lampshade. (*Note:* This material dries in 15–20 minutes, so if you're working on a large shade, you might prefer to work in sections or brush over already-dried areas.)

2. Place the pressed flowers and leaves on the shade in a pleasing scattered arrangement. Use tweezers to make the handling of fragile pieces easier.

3. Brush on a second coat of découpage medium. Let dry.

4. Brush on additional coats of découpage medium until the desired finish is achieved, allowing each coat to dry thoroughly before applying the next.

Herb Wreath

The aroma of an herb garden basking in the hot sun can last long after the season is gone. Fresh herbs hung to dry in the kitchen can flavor fall and winter soups and stews. The wreath shown here was fashioned from herbs noted for both their taste and attractiveness—oregano, rosemary, and sage fresh from the garden—and was allowed to dry naturally into its rounded shape.

SIZE

Wreath shown is 8" in diameter

NATURE'S MATERIALS

Fresh oregano, 12"–16" pieces

Fresh rosemary, 4"–6" pieces

Fresh sage, 4"–6" pieces

SUPPLIES AND TOOLS

2 yards of 1½"-wide sheer multicolor
    ombré ribbon

Fine-gauge floral wire

Wire cutters

Scissors

String

Newspaper

DIRECTIONS

1. Using floral wire, twist a 7"-diameter circle for the wreath base. Wrap pieces of oregano around the wire ring, adding more sprigs and tucking in the ends as you go. The wreath should be quite thick, as it will shrink as it dries. When the wreath is thick and evenly filled out, gently wrap string around it to hold it together until it has dried.

2. Tie 2 small bouquets of rosemary and sage with wire. Place the wreath and the bouquets on newspaper in a dry place away from direct light for 2–3 weeks to dry thoroughly.

3. When the wreath is dry, cut the string and carefully remove it. Cut a yard of ribbon and twine it gently around the wreath, knotting it at the rear top. Wire the 2 bouquets together crosswise. Cut three 10" lengths of ribbon. Cut the ends of the ribbons in inverted V's and stack the ribbons. Twist wire around the center of the ribbon pieces to gather them and wire them to the back of the herbal bouquet. Lay the bouquet across the top of the wreath and secure it with wire. Cover the wire with a 5" piece of ribbon wrapped around the wreath at the top and knotted at the back. Trim the ends.

Lavender Sachets

Dried lavender is a classic filling for sachets and has long been a favorite aroma for bureau drawers and linen closets. Hang these sachets from the hangers among your clothes or tuck them between stacks of clean sheets and towels. Your reward will be the fresh scent of late spring all year long. For instructions and information on drying plant materials see Nature Crafts Basics.

SIZES

Sachets shown are 3"–5"

NATURE'S MATERIALS

For three sachets

Fresh lavender, including flowers, leaves, and stems

Dried lavender for filling

SUPPLIES AND TOOLS

¼ yard of each fabric: lavender gingham, blue gingham, and green gingham; ivory silk organza

3 yards of ⅜"-wide lavender picot-edge satin ribbon

1½ yards of ⅝"-wide sheer multicolor ombré ribbon

Ivory sewing thread

Sewing machine or sewing needle

Template for 9"-diameter circle

Scissors

Hot-glue gun and glue stick

Iron

Ruler

Pencil

Newspaper

DIRECTIONS

1. From fresh lavender, cut and tie with thread 3 tiny 1"–2" bouquets. Place them on newspaper in a warm, dry place away from direct light for 2–3 weeks to dry thoroughly.

2. Make sachets.

   Round: Using the template, draw a 9"-diameter circle on the wrong side of the blue gingham and the organza. Cut the circles out and pin them with right sides together. Stitch the circles using a ¼" seam allowance, leaving a small opening for turning. Trim seam edges and clip curves. Turn right side out and press. Slip-stitch the opening closed. With the organza side facing up, sew 2 rows of gathering stitches 1" from the outside edge. Pull up the gathers. Fill the sachet with dried lavender. Pull the gathering stitches closed and tie off the threads.

   Square: On the wrong side of the green gingham and the organza measure and draw a rectangle 4½" × 11" and cut it out. Pin the rectangles with right sides together. Stitch the rectangles using a ¼" seam allowance, leaving a small opening for turning. Trim the corners, turn right side out, and press. Slipstitch the opening closed. Fold the rectangle in half crosswise, with the organza on the inside, aligning short edges. Sew the side seams. Turn right side out and press. Sew 2 rows of gathering stitches 1½" from the top edge. Pull up the gathers. Fill the sachet with dried lavender. Pull the gathering stitches closed and tie off the threads.

Tube: On the wrong side of the lavender gingham and the organza measure and draw a 7" square and cut it out. Pin the squares with right sides together. Stitch around the square using a ¼" seam allowance, leaving a small opening for turning. Trim the corners, turn right side out, and press. Slipstitch the opening closed. Fold the square in half with the organza on the inside. Stitch along the long edge. Turn the tube right side out. Sew 2 rows of gathering stitches 1½" from the opposite edges of the tube. Pull up the gathers on one end and tie off. Fill the tube with lavender, pull the gathers tight on the opposite end, and tie off.

3. To finish the sachets, cut an 8" piece of satin picot ribbon and tie it around each bag at the gathers. Tie a 3" bow of sheer and picot-edge ribbon around the top of each lavender bouquet. Hot-glue the back of the bouquet to the front of the sachet. Trim the ends of the ribbons on the diagonal. Tack a loop of picot ribbon to the gathers on the back of the round and square sachets for hanging.

Flower-Trimmed Hat

A band of dried flowers from your garden turns a plain straw hat into a fragrant and cheerful bonnet. To intensify the aroma of your favorite flower add a few drops of aromatic oil to the dried materials. Or to discourage insects from buzzing around your head include santolina, tansy, or pennyroyal. Because the band is stitched to the hat, you can replace it with a different one for a seasonal change. For instructions and information on drying flowers and plant materials see Nature Crafts Basics.

SIZE

Straw hat shown has 3" brim

NATURE'S MATERIALS

Dried flowers: red rosebuds, lavender, green-lavender hydrangea, blue larkspur, marigolds
Dried herbs: santolina, sage

SUPPLIES AND TOOLS

Panama-style straw hat with 3" brim
⅔ yard of 1½"-wide grosgrain ribbon in color of choice
Sewing needle
Thread to match ribbon
Hot-glue gun and glue stick

DIRECTIONS

1. Sew the ribbon to the hat around the base of the brim with long straight stitches. Stitch along both edges of the ribbon. The flowers and glue can become heavy enough to pull the ribbon away from the hat, and the stitches will keep it secure and allow you to change the hatband in the future.

2. Hot-glue dried herbs and flowers to the ribbon hatband. Start with one type of herb, distributing it evenly around the hat. Repeat, gluing other varieties of herbs and flowers one at a time, until you have a dense covering. Accent with any extra flowers.

Gourd Birdhouse

The gourd is one of nature's most perfect packages. When it is dried its skin becomes hard and watertight. In ancient times gourds were used as water dippers, bottles, and bowls. A gourd birdhouse provides our feathered friends with a natural shelter that sheds rain and deters predators. Since each species of bird has its own space requirements and prefers a doorway of a certain size, choose the gourd with a particular bird in mind. The titmouse, nuthatch, house wren, and downy woodpecker would be comfortable in the birdhouse shown. Gourds are easy to grow in the garden and are available in the fall at vegetable stands and florists' shops. For instructions and information on drying gourds see Nature Crafts Basics.

SIZE

Birdhouse shown is 10" tall

NATURE'S MATERIALS

Dried gourd
2 lengths of grapevine 3'–4'

SUPPLIES AND TOOLS

Drill, ¼" drill bit, and 1¼"-diameter holesaw
Pruning shears
Hot-glue gun and glue stick

DIRECTIONS

1. Using the holesaw, drill the entrance hole in the center of the gourd. Shake out any loose seeds or dried fiber.

2. Drill two ¼" holes near the top to hold the vine hanger. Drill another hole just below the entrance for a perch. With pruning shears, cut a 3" piece of grapevine and insert it into the hole. Hot-glue the grapevine perch in place so that it will not wiggle.

3. Thread a length of grapevine through the holes in the top of the gourd and tie it in a loop. To make the hanger longer or to add a decorative tangle of vine, thread another length through the first loop and tie it.

4. Hang the birdhouse on a small branch in a tree, above the reach of cats, dogs, and small children.

Dried Citrus Wreath

Citrus fruits—oranges, lemons, limes, and grapefruit—become almost transparent when dried, rather like mottled stained glass. Hung in a window, a citrus wreath will glow with backlight and sunlight. In our version, lemon leaves and moss fill in the areas between the fans of dried citrus slices and provide the background for dried apple slices, pomegranates, red rosebuds, and thyme blossoms. The lemon leaves, wired together when fresh, curl and take on interesting shapes if left to dry naturally on the wreath. For instructions and information on drying fruits see Nature Crafts Basics.

SIZE

Wreath shown is 12" in diameter

NATURE'S MATERIALS

Green Spanish moss

Sheet moss

12 branches (approximately) of lemon leaves

9 dried orange slices ¼" thick

9 dried lime slices ¼" thick

9 dried miniature pomegranates (approximately 2" in diameter)

12 dried apple slices

12 dried rosebuds

12 dried sprigs of thyme blossoms

SUPPLIES AND TOOLS

12"-diameter wire boxed wreath form

Floral wire

Floral tape

Wire cutters

Pruning shears or scissors

Low-temperature glue gun and glue stick

DIRECTIONS

1. Fill in the concave surface of the wreath form with Spanish moss. Wrap it with wire to secure.

2. Soak sheet moss in water to make it flexible. Wrap the wet moss around the entire form and secure it with wire. Let dry thoroughly.

3. From the branches, cut sprigs of lemon leaves with about 3–4 leaves per sprig. Wrap 3–4 sprigs together with floral tape. Using the glue gun, attach the bunches of leaves to the wreath form.

4. Alternate bunches of leaves with clusters of fruit. Arrange the dried citrus slices into 3 circular clusters of 6 overlapping slices. Add 3 clusters of 3 pomegranates. Still using the glue gun, fill in around the citrus and pomegranate clusters with apple slices, bits of Spanish moss, rosebuds, and thyme blossoms. Fill in any empty spaces with lemon leaves.

Pressed-Flower Candles and Floral Candle Wreath

A thin coating of wax will join pressed flowers to plain candles. The wax also intensifies the colors of the dried petals and protects them. Once you are set up with a double boiler of melted wax and a batch of pressed flowers you can quickly decorate a whole box of candles. The accompanying dried floral wreath can be made with pressed or dried pansies and hung on the wall or used as the base for a pillar candle as shown. For instructions and information on drying and pressing plant materials see Nature Crafts Basics.

SIZES

As shown:

Candles include 12" tapers and pillar candle
3" in diameter × 6" high

Wreath is 6" in diameter

NATURE'S MATERIALS

For candles

Pressed flowers and leaves of choice (we
selected Johnny-jump-ups, pansies,
and ferns)

For candle wreath

6"-diameter straw wreath form

Sheet moss

7 dried or pressed pansies

7 dried delphinium blossoms

Dried ferns

8 sprigs of juniper with blue berries

SUPPLIES AND TOOLS

For candles

Candles

Small piece of paraffin or beeswax

Double boiler

Small paintbrush

Tweezers

Waxed paper

For candle wreath

Decorated pillar candle, approximately
3" in diameter × 6" high

Hot-glue gun and glue stick

DIRECTIONS

Candles

1. Spread out waxed paper on the work surface. Unwrap the candles and lay them out with the pressed flowers and the tweezers.

2. Fill the bottom of the double boiler with water and bring it to a boil. Turn the heat down to a simmer. Place wax in the top of the double boiler and cover it. Simmer the water until the wax melts. When the wax is ready, set the double boiler on a trivet on the work surface. You will need to work fairly quickly before the wax cools and begins to harden.

3. Holding a pressed flower with the tweezers, dip it in the melted wax and lay it directly on the candle surface; gently press it onto the candle. Repeat with other pressed flowers and leaves. Put the double boiler back on the stove and reheat the water if the wax starts to harden before you're finished. Keep wax liquid-thin, as a thick layer will have a cloudy look when hard.

4. If there are spots on flowers or leaves not covered with wax, touch them up with the small paintbrush dipped in hot wax. Excess wax can be carefully scraped off with a knife or fingernail.

Wreath

1. Check the fit of the pillar candle in the center of the wreath. You may need to shave the candle base or fill out the wreath form with moss to fit. Wrap the wreath with sheet moss and secure it with hot glue. Work piece by piece, placing a few dots of glue on the wreath and adding pieces of moss to completely cover the wreath form.

2. Glue bits of fern to the moss. Glue pansies, spacing them at even intervals around the wreath. Fill in the spaces between the pansies with delphinium blossoms. Glue juniper sprigs with berries around the top of the inner circumference of the wreath form.

Kitchen Topiaries

Acarefree topiary can be made by attaching dried flowers or any number of decorations to Styrofoam™ forms in the classic topiary shapes of a cone and a sphere. We chose dried herbs and spices appropriate to the kitchen—pepper berries, rose hips, and chili peppers—which were hot-glued to the Styrofoam base mounted on a natural branch. These kitchen ingredients were selected for their size and good looks and are sold for ornamental use, although you could use those packaged for cooking or gather them from the garden and dry them yourself.

SIZES

Left to right as shown (heights include pot):

Chili peppers: 16" tall (cone is 8" tall)

Pepper berries: 17" tall (sphere is 8" in diameter)

Rose hips: 13" tall (sphere is 6" in diameter)

NATURE'S MATERIALS

For one topiary

Sheet moss

Pepper berries, chili peppers, or rose hips

10"–12" branch with bark

SUPPLIES AND TOOLS

Clay flowerpot, 6" in diameter or in size desired

Styrofoam cone or sphere

Plaster of Paris

Disposable container for mixing plaster

Handful of polystyrene packing peanuts or chips

Floral foam

Utility knife

Hot-glue gun and glue stick

Masking tape

DIRECTIONS

1. To make the base, cover the hole in the bottom of the clay pot with masking tape. Cut a 2"-thick block of floral foam to fit snugly in the bottom of the pot. Push the branch into the floral foam so that it can stand up on its own. Sprinkle packing peanuts or chips around the branch to prevent the expanding plaster from cracking the pot as it hardens. Mix the plaster following the manufacturer's directions. Pour it into the pot until about ⅔ full and allow it to set for 24 hours.

2. Fill the rest of the pot with moss and hot-glue a covering of moss around the base of the branch and over the edge of the pot. Push the Styrofoam form onto the branch. Pull it off, apply hot glue to the top of the branch, and replace the form.

3. Make the topiary head of your choice.
   Chili peppers: Hot-glue the peppers around the base of the cone and work in rows toward the top. Glue moss to cover any bare Styrofoam.
   Pepper berries: Hot-glue moss to cover the sphere. Glue pepper berries onto the sphere. Add more pepper berries, making a thick covering while retaining the spherical shape.
   Rose hips: Cover the sphere with rose hips, hot-gluing them close together. Cover any bare Styrofoam with moss.

Eggshell Mosaic Frame

Crushed eggshells colored with natural dyes are the material for fine, small-scale mosaic finishes, ideal for a little wooden box, a miniature tray, or the small picture frame shown here. Because the inner membrane of the egg prevents the shell fragments from adhering with glue, the eggs must be soaked in bleach to remove it before dying. The addition of a little vinegar to the dye may alter the color somewhat, but it enables the dye to penetrate the eggshell. Dye baths can be made from many sources found in the garden (for example, marigold blossoms, red cabbage, beets, daffodils, and delphiniums). For instructions and information on making dyes from natural materials see Nature Crafts Basics.

SIZE

Frame shown is 5¼" square

NATURE'S MATERIALS

3 white uncooked eggs and 1 brown uncooked egg, halved and emptied

3 dyes, 1 made from each of the following: daffodil blossoms, blue delphinium blossoms, and cochineal

SUPPLIES AND TOOLS

5¼"-square picture frame with 2"-square opening or frame of choice with flat surface

Household bleach

White vinegar

Large glass jar to hold bleach solution

3 glass jars for dye baths

4 plates to hold shells of different colors

Spray acrylic sealer

Small, flat paintbrush

Fine sandpaper

Tack cloth

White tacky glue

Tablespoon for measuring

Ruler   Pencil

Paper towels

DIRECTIONS

1. Rinse the eggs thoroughly inside and out with water. Drain them on paper towels and then soak the eggshells in a mild solution of household bleach and water for several hours to dissolve the inner membranes.

2. Make the 3 dyes according to the instructions in Nature Crafts Basics. Pour each color into a separate glass jar to which a tablespoon of white vinegar has been added.

3. Remove the eggshells from the bleach and rinse them thoroughly with fresh water. Dry the shells with paper towels. Place 2 white shell halves in each color dye, reserving the brown eggshell to be used in its natural color. Let the shells sit in the dyes overnight or until they achieve the desired color. Place the shells on paper towels and let them dry completely.

4. Prepare the frame. Sand the front of the frame to remove the glossy finish. Wipe it with the tack cloth. With ruler and pencil, mark off a geometric design, or follow the one in the photograph.

5. Break each eggshell into ½"–¾" pieces and spread each color on its own plate.

6. With the paintbrush, spread glue over a small area of the frame. Work on about 1 square inch at a time. While the glue is wet, press a piece of eggshell against the frame, cracking it with the pressure of your finger. Spread out the fragments to fit within the penciled area. Fill in with little chips where necessary. Leave spaces between the fragments so the color of the frame shows through in the background. Continue until the design is complete. Let dry.

7. Spray with acrylic sealer. Let dry. Sand the edges of the frame to remove any sharp shell edges. Spray again and let dry.

Eggshell Vases

E ggshell vases filled with little nosegays of early spring flowers make perfect favors for an Easter dinner or a birthday party. They can be left uncolored or can be colored when you dye Easter eggs or eggshells for mosaics. Stored in an egg carton, they can be saved for a future occasion or used over and over again. For instructions and information on making dyes from plant materials see Nature Crafts Basics.

SIZE

Determined by eggs of choice

NATURE'S MATERIALS

Chicken, duck, or goose eggs

Dyes made from plant materials

SUPPLIES AND TOOLS

⅝" bone ring (a white plastic ring sold as a sewing notion)

White vinegar

Glass jars for dye baths

Tablespoon for measuring

Hot-glue gun and glue stick

Paper towels

DIRECTIONS

1. Break open the pointed end of each egg and pour out the contents. Wash the eggshells thoroughly inside and out. Turn them upside down on paper towels to dry.

2. Pour each dye into a separate jar to which 1 tablespoon of white vinegar has been added.

3. Immerse the shells in dye. Let them soak overnight or as long as necessary to achieve the desired color. Remove them from the dye and turn them upside down on paper towels to dry.

4. When dry, hot-glue a ⅝" bone ring to the base of each egg.

Citrus Box and Pouch

Experimentation resulted in these two tiny containers made from orange and lemon rinds. The lemon box was made by scooping out the contents of the two halves of a lemon, turning the bottom half inside out, and baking both halves in the oven at a low temperature. They each dried differently—a bit wrinkly and rather amusing. The top half, perched on the bottom half like an elf's hat, becomes the lid. The drawstring pouch is made from half an orange, dried in the same manner, and soft garment-weight leather. The edge of the orange is finished off with beads.

SIZES

As shown:

Lemon box is 2½" tall

Orange and leather pouch is 3" tall

NATURE'S MATERIALS

Lemon or orange

Raw rice

SUPPLIES AND TOOLS

12" square of garment-weight leather or suede

Sinew, ribbon, string, or embroidery floss

Grapefruit spoon or other sharp-sided spoon

2 glass beads, 10 mm, in color of choice

Package of small multicolored beads

X-acto™ knife with #11 blade

Beading needle and thread

Tape measure

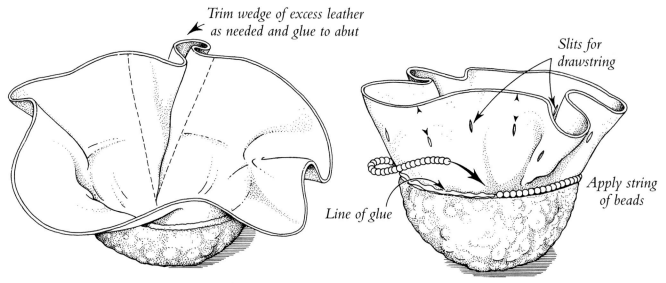

Trim wedge of excess leather as needed and glue to abut

Slits for drawstring

Apply string of beads

Line of glue

Attaching Leather Top to Dried Rind

Scissors

White tacky glue

DIRECTIONS

Lemon Box

Dry a lemon following the directions in the Drying Fruit Rinds box, but turn the bottom half of the lemon inside out. Be careful that you don't tear the rind.

❋ *Drying Fruit Rinds* ❋

Cut the citrus fruit in half and scoop out all the pulp with a grapefruit spoon, leaving some of the white inner rind. Cut a thin sliver off each end so the halves stand relatively upright. Place the halves on a baking sheet, fill each with uncooked rice to keep the shape, and bake in a preheated 175° oven for 4 hours or until the rinds are very hard. You can also put them on top of a radiator or wood stove that is constantly warm, although it will take longer for the rinds to dry and harden by this method. When the rinds are dry and hard, remove them from the oven and let them cool. Discard the rice.

Orange Pouch

1. Dry an orange half following the directions in the Drying Fruit Rinds box.

2. On the piece of leather draw a circle whose diameter is equal to the circumference of the dried orange. With sharp scissors cut out the circle

3. Coat the inside of the dried rind with white tacky glue. Push the center of the leather circle into the base of the rind and press it down so it adheres. There will be some excess: Make a wedge-shaped cut into the leather, cut away the extra leather, and glue down the raw edges so they butt against each other.

4. Using the X-acto knife, cut a series of vertical slits for the drawstring about ½" down from the top edge of the leather and 1" apart. Lace a piece of sinew, ribbon, string, or embroidery floss though the slits. Finish off the ends with 2 glass beads.

5. Measure the circumference of the pouch where the rind and the leather join. Make a string of tiny colored beads to this measurement. Spread a thin line of glue around the outer rim of the rind where it meets the leather and glue on the string of beads. Let dry.

Seed-Covered Birdhouses

These charming, delicate birdhouses are meant for indoor viewing and habitation by imaginary birds. Slip a couple in among a collection of baskets atop rustic kitchen cabinets or nestle one under a lamp on a living room table. Made of balsa wood and basswood, the construction is lightweight and easy. Roofs and trim are painted in bright colors, and the textured walls consist of ordinary birdseed from the grocery store.

SIZES

Green-roof birdhouse is 5" wide × 3½" deep × 5" high

Red-roof birdhouse is 3½" wide × 2⅛" deep × 7¼" high

Blue-roof birdhouse is 3⅜" wide × 3¼" deep × 8" high

NATURE'S MATERIALS

Birdseed: thistle; sunflower; and wild-bird seed mix (mostly millet)

2 small twigs with bark for perch, approximately 1½" long

SUPPLIES AND TOOLS

1 piece of ¼" balsa wood 3" × 24"

4 pieces of ³⁄₃₂" basswood 3" × 24"

1 piece of ½" spacing basswood clapboard siding 3¼" × 24"

Wood glue

Acrylic paint: phthalocyanine blue, phthalocyanine green, cadmium red medium, cadmium red light, cadmium yellow medium, black

Template for 1½"-diameter circle

X-acto knife with #11 blade

Paintbrush

Fine sandpaper

Ruler

Pencil

DIRECTIONS

1. Patterns shown are one-half actual size. With a pencil and a ruler draw patterns full size on the wood specified in the Birdhouse Cutting Guide, using the measurements given on the patterns. Where a pattern says "cut 2," draw 2 on the wood.

2. With an X-acto knife and a ruler, cut out the pieces.

❈ Birdhouse ❈ Cutting Guide

From ¼" balsa wood

base of green-roof birdhouse: cut 1; ¼" strips, cut 4

base of red-roof birdhouse: cut 1

From ³⁄₃₂" basswood

base of blue-roof birdhouse: cut 1

sides of all birdhouses: cut 2 for each house

front and backs of all birdhouses: cut 2 for each house; on each front, mark and cut out the 1½"-diameter circle where indicated

From basswood clapboard

roofs: cut 2 each for red and green; cut 1 for blue

Sides and roofs are pieced as needed. Sand pieces after cutting as needed.

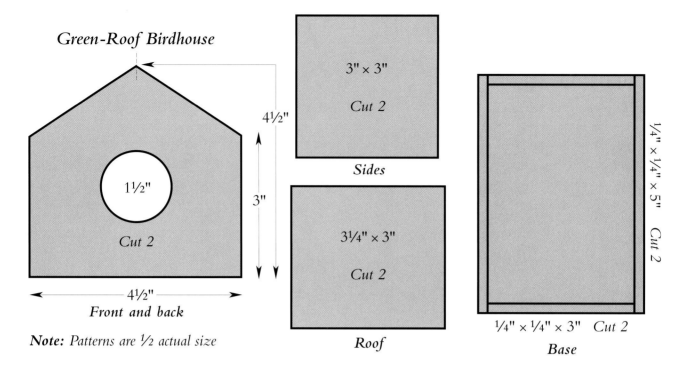

Green-Roof Birdhouse

Sides — 3" × 3" Cut 2

Roof — 3¼" × 3" Cut 2

¼" × ¼" × 5" Cut 2

¼" × ¼" × 3" Cut 2

Base

Front and back — 4½", 4½", 3", 1½" Cut 2

Note: Patterns are ½ actual size

Green-Roof Birdhouse

1. Glue the ¼" strips to the sides of the base.

2. Mix dark brown paint using cadmium red medium, green, and black. Thin it with water and "stain" the house walls on both sides. Let dry. Thin the green paint and "stain" the roof and the base. Rub cadmium red light paint on the inside edge of the entrance hole.

3. Glue the sides to the front. Glue on the back. Glue the roof and the base in place. Let the glue dry.

4. Starting at the bottom, glue the sunflower seeds, with the rounded ends down, to the sides of the birdhouse, like shingles, covering all the walls except for a ¼"-wide ring around the hole and a bare spot for the twig perch just below the hole. Let the glue dry. Glue the wild-bird seed mix around the hole. Glue the twig perch in place.

Red-Roof Birdhouse

Note: Patterns are ½ actual size

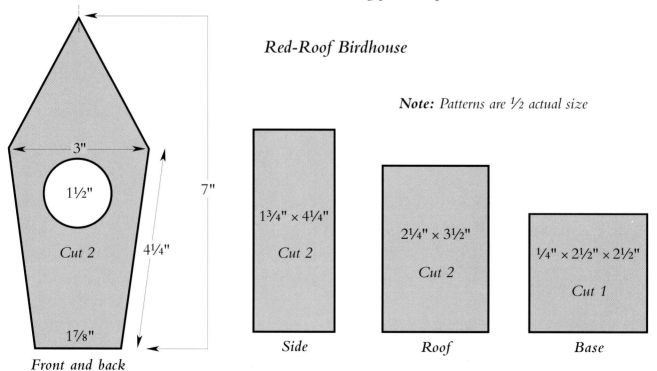

Front and back — 3", 1½", 7", 4¼", 1⅞" Cut 2

Side — 1¾" × 4¼" Cut 2

Roof — 2¼" × 3½" Cut 2

Base — ¼" × 2½" × 2½" Cut 1

Blue-Roof Birdhouse

Note: Patterns are ½ actual size

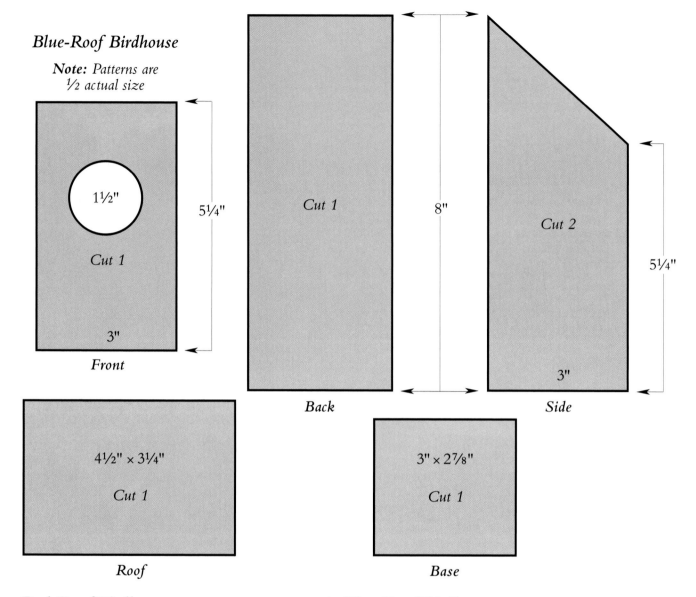

1½"

5¼"

Cut 1

3"

Front

Cut 1

8"

Cut 2

5¼"

3"

Back

Side

4½" × 3¼"

Cut 1

Roof

3" × 2⅞"

Cut 1

Base

Red-Roof Birdhouse

1. "Stain" the inside of the birdhouse with dark brown paint, mixed according to the instructions in step 2 on page 38. Mix a little brown with cadmium red light and add water. "Stain" the outside of the birdhouse, roof, and base. Let dry. "Antique" the roof and the base by dry-brushing dark brown paint along the edges. Paint the inside of the hole with yellow.

2. Glue the front, back, and sides of the birdhouse together. Glue the roof and the base to the sides and allow the glue to dry.

3. Working on one side at a time, spread an even coat of glue on the birdhouse and cover with thistle seed. Shake lightly to remove excess seeds. Let dry and repeat for the other sides.

Blue-Roof Birdhouse

1. "Stain" the roof with phthalocyanine blue. Paint the inside of the hole with cadmium red medium.

2. Glue the birdhouse front, back, and sides to the base. Add the roof and allow the glue to dry.

3. Working on one side at a time, spread an even coat of glue on the birdhouse and cover with wild-bird seed mix, leaving bare a ½"-wide ring around the hole and a spot for the twig perch just below the hole. Shake lightly to remove the excess seeds. Let dry. Glue sunflower seeds around the hole, with the small ends pointed inward. Glue the twig perch in place. Fill in around the perch and hole with glue and wild-bird seed mix as needed.

Seed Embroidery

In a pattern straight from Fabergé, the famed jeweler to the czars, pumpkin, cantaloupe, and honeydew melon seeds are worked with brightly colored wooden beads on linen fabric in a design that belies their origin. Seed embroidery can be worked on apparel, framed and hung on a wall, or set into the top of an oak box intended for needlework, as shown here. Follow the pattern and use the suggested materials or try other seeds, perhaps black watermelon seeds with seed pearls. For instructions and information on drying seeds see Nature Crafts Basics.

SIZE

Box shown is 9" square

NATURE'S MATERIALS

1 cup of dried honeydew melon seeds

½ cup of dried pumpkin seeds

½ cup of dried cantaloupe seeds

SUPPLIES AND TOOLS

½ yard of dark green fabric (we used Lugana™ by Zweigart) or any solid-color fabric

9"-square finished oak box with 7¼" design insert in lid

12"-square wooden needlepoint frame or artist's stretcher and pushpins

Wooden beads:

    1 large orange bead for center

    1 yellow bead for center, 8 mm

    8 magenta beads, 8 mm

    8 pale yellow oblong beads

    52 rust-colored beads, 6 mm

    20 magenta beads, 6 mm

    ½ cup of yellow beads, 4 mm

Glass beads:

    4 orange beads, 8 mm

    8 magenta beads, 4 mm

6" square of felt

8" square of polyester quilt batting

4 size 10 beading needles

Size 7 or 8 sewing needle

Yellow, orange, magenta, and ecru cotton-covered sewing thread

White basting thread

Straight pins

Thimble

Scissors

Beeswax

8" square of paper

Pencil

Terry washcloth

Steam iron

DIRECTIONS

1. Iron the fabric to remove any creases and mount it in the needlepoint frame or stretcher, pulling the fabric taut before tightening the frame or while pinning in place.

2. Transfer the pattern onto 8"-square paper. Pin the paper design to the fabric, aligning the design with the grain of the fabric. With the sewing needle and white thread, baste through the paper and the fabric around the outside edge of the design. Mark the locations of the center crossing lines and the surrounding X's and dots with thread. To do this, push

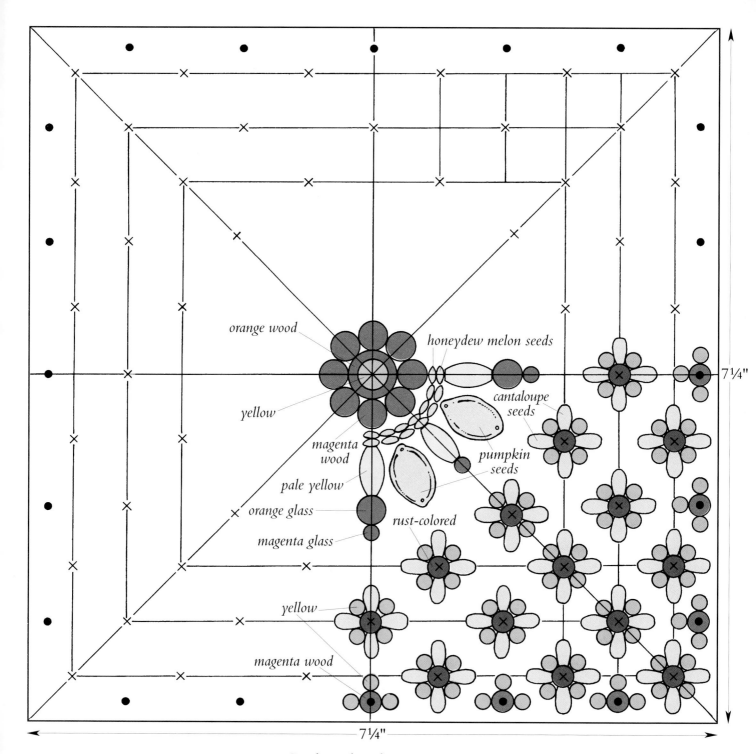

orange wood

honeydew melon seeds

yellow

cantaloupe seeds

magenta wood

pumpkin seeds

pale yellow

orange glass

rust-colored

magenta glass

yellow

magenta wood

7¼"

7¼"

Seed Embroidery Pattern

pins straight down through the paper and fabric. Carefully remove the paper. Make white thread X marks at the location of each pin.

3. Use thread to match the beads, waxed with beeswax, throughout. Have a beading needle threaded in each of the 4 colors to save time. With the photograph and pattern

as guides, attach the large orange wooden bead with the 8-mm yellow wooden bead on top. Knot securely and clip on the wrong side of the fabric. Attach eight 8-mm magenta wooden beads around the large orange bead. Attach 8 pale yellow oblong beads.

4. Attach 4 orange glass beads at the ends of 4 of the just-attached pale yellow oblong

beads. Attach 8 magenta glass beads to ends of the remaining pale yellow oblong beads and to the 4 orange glass beads.

5. Make a hole in each end of the dried pumpkin seeds: Fold a soft pad of the felt, place the seed on it, and, using a thimble to protect your finger, push a sharp sewing needle through the seed. The felt prevents the seed from cracking when you press down on it with the needle. Attach 8 pumpkin seeds between the pale yellow oblong seeds by tacking through the hole at each end.

6. Following the instructions for making holes in seeds in step 5, make a hole at the pointed end of each honeydew melon seed and then stitch a double row of honeydew melon seeds between the row of magenta beads and the row of pale yellow oblong beads and pumpkin seeds. The honeydew seeds should stand up or lean at an angle rather than lie flat.

7. Attach a 6-mm rust-colored wooden bead at the center of all the X's stitched on the fabric.

8. With sharp scissors, snip a tiny bit off the end of each cantaloupe seed and then poke holes at both ends as described in step 5. With the cut ends against the orange beads, attach 4 cantaloupe seeds equidistant around each 6-mm rust-colored wooden bead. Finish each motif by attaching four 4-mm yellow wooden beads between the melon seeds pulled up close to the rust-colored center bead.

9. Finish the border of the design by attaching the 6-mm magenta wooden beads at the outside row of dots and then surrounding each one with three 4-mm yellow wooden beads as shown.

10. To set the threads on the back of the embroidery, wrap a hot iron with a damp terry washcloth. Hold the iron 2" below the wrong side of the embroidery (still in the needlework frame) and let the steam filter up through the fabric. Professional embroiderers often finish beaded works by lightly touching each knot with watered-down white glue or gum arabic. This is important for beading done on garments, which will have to withstand wear, but is not necessary for this project.

11. Place a layer of quilt batting under the embroidery design. Mount the design and batting in the oak box insert, following the manufacturer's instructions.

Handmade Note Paper, Gift Boxes, and Bookmark

Colorful, scented handmade papers tinted and textured with flowers and leaves from your own garden will make a note or gift particularly special. Coloring and scenting the paper are as easy as brewing tea. Herb infusions such as lemon verbena, mint, rosemary, thyme, and cloves will add a delicate scent. Some can be used as tints as well; lemon verbena, for example, will produce a cream color and rose hips a reddish pink. Fragments of sheer fabric, embroidery floss, or flakes of gold leaf will add variety to the texture. For instructions and information on making paper and on drying and pressing plant materials, see Nature Crafts Basics. Experiment to create your own variations.

SIZES

As shown:

Sheets of paper are 7" × 10"

Paper boxes are 3½" × 8½"

Bookmark is 2½" × 7"

NATURE'S MATERIALS

Dried and pressed flowers and leaves for handmade paper

SUPPLIES AND TOOLS

Ribbon: picot-edged satin, velvet, or sheer colors with gold edges as shown, or ribbons of choice; for tying gift boxes, 1¼ yards; for bookmark, 6"

Small paintbrush

Hole punch

Dinner knife or other blunt knife

Scissors

White tacky glue

Ruler

Pencil

DIRECTIONS

Note Paper

Following the instructions in Nature Crafts Basics, make sheets of note paper. For note cards, fold handmade paper sheets in half.

Gift Box

1. Using the box pattern on page 47 as a model, make a pattern to the dimensions shown or to the size desired and transfer it to the wrong side of a piece of handmade paper. Cut out the box form. Score and crease along the fold lines with the blunt side of a dinner knife.

2. Spread a thin layer of glue on the right side of the paper tab and then glue it to the wrong side of the opposite edge of the paper. This will form an invisible side seam.

3. Wrap the gift in tissue paper and slip it into the box. At each side, fold down the curved ends, one over the other. Cut a 1-yard length of ribbon, wrap it around the box in both directions, and tie a bow. Clip the ribbon ends as desired.

Bookmark

1. Fold a sheet of handmade paper about 2½" from the 7" end. Gently tear along the fold

THE GARDENS.

CANTO THE SECOND.

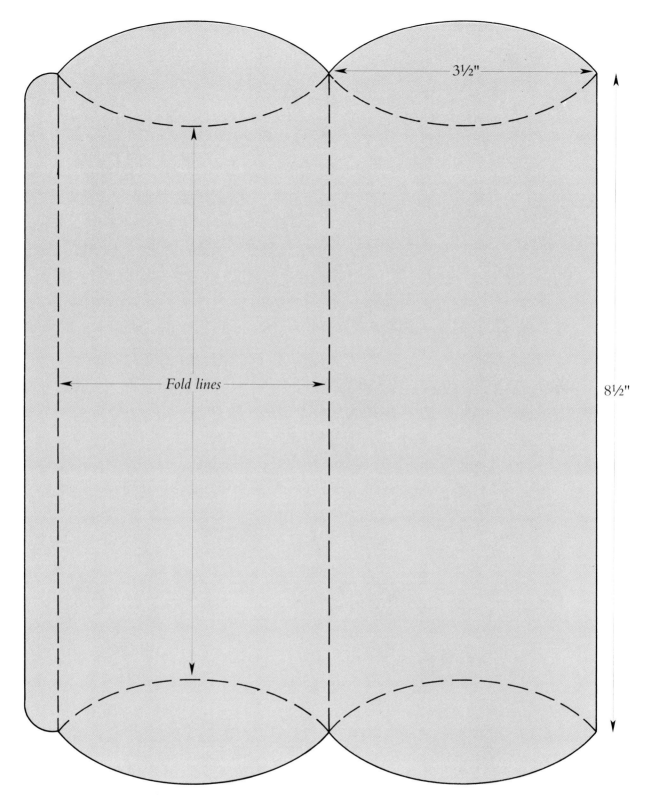

3½"

8½"

Fold lines

Handmade-Paper Gift Box Pattern

line. Do not cut with scissors or the edge will be too sharp. Repeat with paper of another color, making this piece ½" shorter and narrower than the first. Brush a light coating of white glue on the wrong side of the smaller piece, center it, and glue it to the right side of the larger.

2. Punch a hole at the top. Cut a 6" length of ribbon, slip it through the hole, and tie it.

Woodlands

A casual stroll through a farmer's woodlot, a nature preserve, or an urban park will open your eyes to nature's incredible bounty. The variety of materials that "grow on trees" is remarkable: leaves of all shapes, colors, and sizes; bark of many textures covered with fantastical curling lichen; twigs, straight and sleek or gnarled and spiky; and all sorts of nuts, acorns, and seedpods. Strange and otherworldly materials, such as fungi, may be discovered at the base of a rotting stump or hidden beneath a carpet of leaves. The woodland crafts projects that follow require small quantities of materials, and if you harvest wisely, taking a little bit from each plant or area, the woods will soon replenish its stock.

For projects made with bark, collect your material only from fallen branches or from logs on the woodpile. Never remove bark from a living tree, as an open wound will inhibit the tree's circulation and make it susceptible to infection. Girdling a tree—that is, removing the bark in a complete band around the trunk—will kill it.

Nature's gifts are plentiful. A woodland walk is certain to yield other exotic materials not mentioned here that will make your nature crafts projects truly unique.

Maple Leaf Roses

A bouquet of summer-green maple leaves collected on a warm afternoon walk will turn into rose-shaped clusters when tied together and left to dry. The leaves curl as they dry, overlapping one another much like the petals of a rose. They will stay green for several months, with more intense color toward their centers. Heaped in a basket and interspersed with dried hydrangeas, they make an arrangement that is rich in texture and color. Later in the year gather leaves that have turned yellow, orange, and red to make "roses" for a spectacular autumn display. For instructions and information on drying flowers see Nature Crafts Basics. For instructions on making the vine basket shown in the photo see page 88.

SIZES

Each rose shown is approximately 6" in diameter

NATURE'S MATERIALS

For one rose

12–15 large maple leaves (for best results make roses within 12 hours of picking leaves)

SUPPLIES AND TOOLS

Fine-gauge floral wire
Wire cutters

DIRECTIONS

1. Choose 3 leaves for the center. Fold each leaf in half vertically and then vertically in half again. Gather them into a bouquet, holding them together a little above the bases of the leaves.

2. Add the other leaves to the bouquet by wrapping them around the first 3 leaves. As you add each leaf, turn the bouquet so the leaves are staggered to create petals. To vary the colors, alternate the sides of the leaves so that the right side faces in and then out. Keep pinching the bases of the leaves together as you work. When dry, they will curl in and out like flower petals.

3. When you have added as many leaves as you wish, wrap floral wire around the bottom of the leaves just above your fingers. Work gently so the wire does not cut the leaves. There's no need to wrap the stems.

4. Place each rose upright in a cup or glass to dry. Leave in a warm, dry place for 1–2 weeks. (In summer a hot attic is a good place for drying.)

Oak Leaf Wreath

Oak leaves, often overlooked and underappreciated because they are so common, come in an astonishing range of shapes and sizes, from tiny leaves with scalloped edges that dry a pale parchment color to huge, spiky leaves that turn rich brown and measure a foot long. The leaves used in this vibrant wreath are from the pin oak. To make this wreath use either leaves you have collected or preserved leaves, which you can buy from your local florist or a craft supply store. They are available in white, yellow, orange, and dark green. The natural leaves will be a bit more brittle to work with, but their colors and textures will be unusual and beautiful. For instructions and information on preserving and drying plant materials see Nature Crafts Basics.

SIZE

Wreath shown is 18" in diameter

NATURE'S MATERIALS

Spanish moss

Several dozen twigs of oak leaves, fresh or preserved

Dried hydrangea blossoms and leaves

Large acorns

Miniature pomegranates

Pinecones

Bittersweet vine

SUPPLIES AND TOOLS

18"-diameter wire boxed wreath form

Gold felt-tip paint marker

Floral wire

Brown floral tape

Pruning shears

Wire cutters

Scissors

Hot-glue gun and glue stick

DIRECTIONS

1. Fill the wire wreath form with Spanish moss and wrap with floral wire to secure it.

2. From the twigs cut sprigs of oak with 4–5 leaves per sprig and wrap them with floral tape into bunches of 5–6 sprigs. Make up about 16 bunches.

3. Place 1 bunch on the wreath form and tie the stems to the form with floral wire. Overlap the first bunch with the next and wire it to secure. Continue around the wreath until it is entirely covered. Arrange the leaves, fluffing them out as necessary.

4. Dab the tips of the acorns with the gold felt-tip marker to make them stand out against the leaves.

5. Arrange 5 clusters of hydrangea evenly around the wreath. Spread the oak leaves apart and hot-glue the clusters to the wreath form. Glue acorns, pomegranates, pinecones, and tendrils of bittersweet around the hydrangeas as desired.

Stenciled Leaf Tray

Leaves have ideal shapes for stenciling with spray paint. Press the leaves for a few days in a flower press or a large phone book so that they lie flat, providing a well-defined outline. You may also want to consider using blades of grass and flower heads as stencils, combined with complementary paint colors. The gold edging on the tray introduces another craft—gilding. The same stenciling and gilding techniques described in this project can be used on wooden boxes and plaques, on the backs of breadboards, and on metal or other hard surfaces. For instructions and information on pressing leaves see Nature Crafts Basics.

SIZE

Tray shown is 16" wide × 21" long × 2" high

NATURE'S MATERIALS

Pressed leaves of choice (we used oak, maple, gingko, and birch)

SUPPLIES AND TOOLS

Wooden tray

Acrylic spray paint: golden yellow, barn red, and green

White oil-based primer (if tray is unfinished wood)

1–2 sheets of composition gold leaf

2-ounce jar of gold-leaf adhesive size

Small jar of umber antiquing gel

Acrylic spray sealer

Sandpaper, medium and fine

Tack cloth

Soft cloth

1/2"-wide paintbrush

Masking tape

Scissors

Newspaper

DIRECTIONS

1. Prepare the tray surface for painting. Sand with medium and then fine sandpaper to remove the finish. Wipe with a tack cloth. If the tray is unfinished wood, paint with white oil-based primer. Let dry.

2. Spread newspaper over a wide area, because sprayed paint will float on the air. Place the tray in the center of the newspaper and, following manufacturer's instructions, spray yellow and red, alternating the areas of color and overlapping them slightly to blend. Cover the floor of the tray with color. The rim and back will be painted after the stencils are applied. Let dry thoroughly.

3. Arrange pressed leaves on the tray surface and tape the backs of the leaves to the tray with small pieces of folded masking tape. (This keeps the leaves from blowing about when you spray on the paint.) Spray green paint over the leaves and on the rim of the tray. Hold the spray can directly above the leaves to get the sharpest stenciled edges. Let dry thoroughly.

4. Turn the tray over and spray-paint the sides and the back green. Let dry thoroughly.

5. Remove the leaves to reveal the stenciled pattern.

6. To gild the rim of the tray, use the paintbrush to apply a thin coat of gold-leaf adhesive size all around. As it dries it will change from milky to clear. Cut ½" strips of composition gold leaf. When the size is completely clear (after about an hour), apply the gold leaf. Press each piece onto the size with a soft cloth. Allow cracks and uneven spaces between the pieces of gold leaf for a casual, worn look. Burnish the gold leaf with the soft cloth to smooth it out, press down wrinkles, and polish it. After the size has dried and cured for at least 12 hours, brush on umber antiquing gel to soften the color of the edges of the gilding. Let dry thoroughly.

7. Spray the tray with several light coats of sealer, following the manufacturer's instructions.

Stenciled Leaf Napkin and Gilded Acorn Napkin Ring

A touch of gold leaf on a real acorn adds a hint of elegance to a humble grapevine napkin ring, shown on page 56 encircling a muslin napkin adorned with the same spray-painted stencils as are used in the Stenciled Leaf Tray on page 53. The painted napkin is set with a warm iron to make it washable. All sorts of pods, seeds, and nuts can be used to decorate the napkin ring, but extremely fragile leaves or flowers should be avoided. The oak leaves on the napkin ring were preserved with glycerine to make them longer lasting and less brittle than dried leaves. For instructions and information on working with grapevine and on preserving and pressing plant materials see Nature Crafts Basics.

SIZES

As shown:

Napkin is 19" square
Napkin ring is 3" in diameter

NATURE'S MATERIALS

For napkin

Pressed oak and maple leaves (or leaves of choice)

For napkin ring

Large acorn
3" grapevine ring (purchased or handmade)
4–5 preserved oak leaves

SUPPLIES AND TOOLS

For napkin

Napkin, 100% cotton muslin
Acrylic spray paint: golden yellow and green
Masking tape   Iron
Newspaper

For napkin ring

Composition gold leaf
Gold-leaf adhesive size
Soft cloth
Small paintbrush
Hot-glue gun and glue stick

DIRECTIONS

Napkin

1. Wash and iron the napkin.

2. Spread newspaper over a wide work area, as sprayed paint will float on the air.

3. Lay the napkin face up on the newspaper. Arrange a maple leaf at one corner of the napkin and tape its back to the napkin with a small piece of folded masking tape. Spray gently with yellow paint, making a cloud of color around the edges of the leaf. Leave the maple leaf in place. Let the paint dry thoroughly.

4. Place oak leaves on either side of the maple leaf and tape them to the napkin as above.

Spray lightly with green paint. Let dry 5 minutes. Remove the leaves. Iron the back of the napkin to set the paint.

Napkin Ring

1. Gently pull off the acorn cap. Brush gold-leaf adhesive size onto the base of the acorn. When the size has turned from milky to clear, lay a small piece of composition gold leaf on the acorn and gently rub or burnish with the soft cloth. Hot-glue the cap back onto the acorn.

2. Glue the acorn to the center front of the grapevine ring.

3. Glue the preserved leaves around the top of the acorn.

Bark Berry Basket

The next time you're out for a walk, gather little pieces of bark from fallen limbs to transform a berry basket with woodland whimsy. You'll be surprised by the variety of colors and textures of bark and the different types of lichen that grow on them. The more varieties of bark, the more interesting the texture of the basket becomes. In winter peruse the woodpile for unusual materials. Trim the basket with a band of dried sheet moss from the florist shop and fill it with your choice of dried flowers. Dried red roses and leaves are tucked tightly into the basket shown here. For instructions and information on drying flowers and leaves see Nature Crafts Basics.

SIZE

Berry basket shown is 6" square × 3½" high

NATURE'S MATERIALS

1 dozen dried red roses or other flowers
  with leaves
Scraps of bark in a variety of colors and
  textures
Dried lichen
Sheet moss

SUPPLIES AND TOOLS

Quart-size wooden berry basket
Floral foam
Hot-glue gun and glue stick

DIRECTIONS

1. Using the hot-glue gun, cover the basket with bark piece by piece. Embellish the basket with lichen or other interesting materials from the woods.

2. Tear the moss into thin strips and glue it around the rim of the basket.

3. Cut floral foam to fit the basket about 1" below the rim. Make a low arrangement of dried flowers by inserting the stems into the foam.

❀ Collecting Natural ❀ Materials

Gather the materials for nature crafts projects as efficiently as possible. When cutting branches or twigs, use sharp pruning shears to minimize damage to the tree and cut sparingly and at random. Cut from several trees to lessen the impact on any one plant. Faster-growing species, such as the willow, will recover more quickly than slower-growing ones. A good source for straight and flexible branches is the suckers that sprout from the base of the trunk or the stump of a recently felled tree. For small amounts of bark look for fallen branches or check the woodpile. Never cut bark from a living tree; the wound will slow the tree's circulation and invite infection. Girdling a tree (cutting the bark from around the trunk) will kill it.

Bark Wall Pocket

A decorative bark wall pocket can be filled with dried flowers and hung on the wall or used as a cornucopia centerpiece filled with fruits, nuts, or dried flowers. This project takes advantage of white birch bark's light weight, flexibility, and natural tendency to curl. If you cannot find a large sheet of bark, make a cone out of poster board and hot-glue fragments of bark to cover it.

SIZE

Wall pocket shown is 13" long × 4" in diameter

NATURE'S MATERIALS

1 sheet of white birch bark about 12" square or scraps of bark (to be glued to a cone of poster board)

Sheet moss

Dried flowers and plants (we used hydrangea blossoms, ammobium, roses, amaranth, wild grasses, a sunflower, and dried ivy)

SUPPLIES AND TOOLS

12" square of white poster board (if large piece of bark is not available)

Floral wire

Floral foam

Drill and 1/16" drill bit (or other tool to make holes in bark)

Wire cutters

Utility knife

Hot-glue gun and glue stick

DIRECTIONS

1. Roll the sheet of bark into a cone and hot-glue along the outer flap to hold it in place, or coil the poster board into a cone and glue it. Cover the cone with small scraps of bark, hot-gluing them on much like a patchwork. Use little tufts of moss to fill in any gaps.

2. Tear thin strips of moss and hot-glue them along the seams and around the top front edge of the cone. Dress up the cone by hot-gluing on a strand of dried ivy if desired.

3. Drill or poke 2 small holes in the top back of the cone. Loop a piece of floral wire through the holes and twist the ends to make a hanger.

4. Cut a piece of floral foam to fit inside the mouth of the cone. Add the dried flowers in a pleasing arrangement by inserting the stems into the foam.

Branch Table Lamp

Three branches and a short section of a small log is all it takes to make the base of a rustic lamp for desk or dresser. The electrical parts can be assembled at the hardware store, and the shade is the clip-on type, made of brown paper. If desired, decorate the shade with pressed flowers as shown on page 19. A twig hot-glued to the top of the shade becomes a finial. The wood used here is gray birch.

SIZE

Lamp shown is 28" high, including finial

NATURE'S MATERIALS

7"–8" length of log, 2" in diameter

3 branches about 18" long

2' strand of grapevine

Twig

SUPPLIES AND TOOLS

6" length of ⅛" IP (international pipe) ⅜"-OD (outside diameter) threaded pipe

2½" length of ½"-OD brass tubing to fit over the ⅜" threaded pipe

Brass neck ⅞" high, slip ⅛" IP

Brass knurled locknut

Socket with turn knob

6' of brown plastic-covered #18 parallel electrical cord

Wire staple (brown if possible)

Male plug

Clip-on paper lampshade, tent-shaped, 14" in diameter

Drill and ⅜" drill bit (long enough to drill through 6" log if possible) and drill bit slightly smaller than diameter of finishing nails

1½" finishing nails

Hacksaw for cutting threaded pipe and brass tube if necessary

Wood saw for cutting log and branches

Loppers or pruning shears for cutting branches

Hammer

Wire cutters and stripper

Long-nosed pliers

Small screwdriver

Utility knife

Hot-glue gun and glue stick

Lightbulb

DIRECTIONS

1. With the wood saw, cut the log into a 6" length overall with a flat top and an angled bottom as shown in the diagram. Using the ⅜" bit, drill through the length of the log. (If your bit is not long enough to drill the whole 6", you will have to drill from both ends.)

2. Arrange the branches in a tripod around the log; mark their positions. Using the bit slightly smaller than the finishing nails, drill through each branch near the top. Attach the 3 branch legs to the log where previously marked, by nailing them in place with the finishing nails. Cut the ends of the legs at an angle with the loppers or the pruning shears so the lamp base stands straight.

3. Twist the threaded pipe about 2" into the hole in the center of the lamp base. Slip the 2½" length of brass tubing over the pipe, leaving about 1½" of threaded pipe exposed above the tubing. Using the diagram as a guide, slip on the brass neck, then screw on the knurled locknut and the base of the socket.

4. Thread the electrical cord through the threaded pipe and the log. Hammer in the wire staple to secure the wire to the bottom of the log. At the top, split the end of the wire in half for about 1½". Strip off ¾" of the plastic covering from the ends of the wire. Assemble the socket following the manufacturer's instructions. Use the long-nosed pliers to twist the ends of the bare wire before slipping them around the contact screws on the socket.

5. Following the manufacturer's instructions, attach the male plug at the end of the electrical cord.

6. Wrap the length of grapevine around the top of the lamp legs and tuck the ends inside the strands to hold it in place.

7. Cut a 5" or 6" length of twig and hot-glue it to the top of the clip-on lampshade for a finial.

8. Screw the lightbulb into the socket and clip the shade to the bulb.

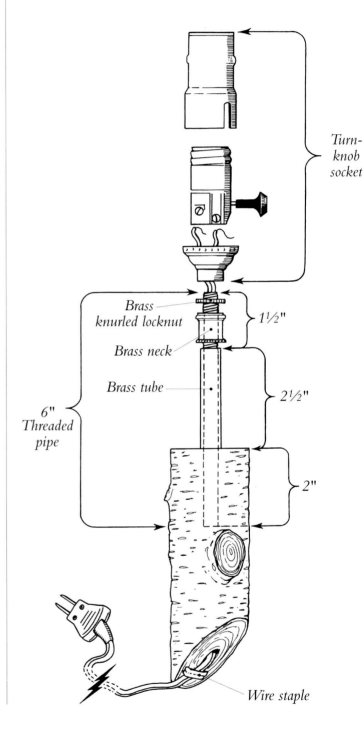

Branch Table Lamp Construction Diagram

Turn-knob socket

Brass knurled locknut

Brass neck

Brass tube

6" Threaded pipe

1½"

2½"

2"

Wire staple

Twig Torchères

The natural curving, forking tendencies of twigs make these candleholders especially amusing. Use any wood that is handy. These are a combination of birch and poplar, but any twigs downed by the wind, sprouts that have intruded into a hedge, or prunings from a fruit tree will all do fine. A variety of bark colors and textures will make the torchères more interesting. The candles shown are made from rolled honeycomb beeswax. Column candles in warm earth colors would also be handsome.

SIZES

Torchères shown are 7", 8", and 10" tall × 5¼" in diameter

NATURE'S MATERIALS

For 3 torchères

1 branch approximately 15" long × ¾" in diameter

Assorted branching twigs up to 12" long (3 needed for each torchère)

SUPPLIES AND TOOLS

3 plywood circles ¼" thick × 4¾" in diameter

1"-long panel nails

Acrylic paint: red and pumpkin

3 candles 3"–4" in diameter

Power jigsaw

Drill and drill bit slightly smaller in diameter than panel nails

Hammer

Pruning shears

Paintbrush

DIRECTIONS

1. For each torchère select 3 branching twigs and arrange them in a tripod. Attach the first twig leg to a plywood circle by drilling and nailing through the plywood and into the top of the twig. Attach the other 2 twig legs in the same way. Trim the ends with pruning shears so the torchère will stand level. Repeat for other torchères.

2. Apply a coat of red paint to the plywood circles. Let dry. Repeat with a rough coat of pumpkin color, using a brush with very little paint to allow some of the red to show through. Let dry.

3. Using the jigsaw, cut the ¾"-diameter branch on the diagonal, into oval discs about ¼" thick.

4. Nail the discs to the edges of the plywood circles using the panel nails.

5. Place a candle in the center of each torchère.

Branch Birdbath

The glimmer of water in the garden is a great attraction for wild birds. This rustic branch birdbath will look right at home surrounded by pachysandra ground cover in a shady spot or at the center of a geometrically laid-out herb garden. Keep the birdbath in the open to prevent surprise attacks by lurking cats but still handy to a nearby branch for birds' preening and sunning. A large clay saucer, such as those used with terra-cotta flowerpots, set between the branches of the base serves as the basin and can be removed easily and scrubbed clean. Frequent water changes are necessary to prevent the spread of disease and to keep the birds happy. Since the branches are irregular, you will have to improvise and fit the pieces together like a puzzle; an extra pair of hands will make the assembly easier.

SIZE

Birdbath shown is 30" high

NATURE'S MATERIALS

3–4 fallen tree limbs (we used oak) approximately 4' long × 2" in diameter, with branches, bark, and lichen left in place

3–6 smaller limbs for cross braces

SUPPLIES AND TOOLS

Clay saucer to fit tripod base

2½"–3" multipurpose screws with Phillips head

Screw gun or screwdriver

Drill and drill bit slightly smaller in diameter than screws

Pruning saw

DIRECTIONS

1. Have a helper hold the saucer at the desired height. Arrange the 3 limbs around the saucer in a rough tripod shape and decide on the location of the center of the tripod. Cut the limbs to the desired length, sawing the ends on the diagonal as shown in the photograph.

2. Reassemble the 3 pieces and, while your helper is holding them in place, drill a hole through all the pieces at the intersection (see diagram A on page 66 as a guide). Screw the tripod together.

3. Cut 3 smaller limbs to fit between the 3 legs of the tripod (see diagram B on page 66 for placement). These cross braces will serve as the platform for the saucer. Place one end of each cross brace next to the inside of a leg and the other end next to the outside of the next leg. Cut the ends on the diagonal. Drill holes in the cross braces and screw them to the tripod legs.

4. Add any other pieces to fill out the overall composition or to give the tripod base more support. The birdbath shown has a fourth leg and a cross brace added to the tripod to make it sturdier.

5. Position the clay saucer securely on the base.

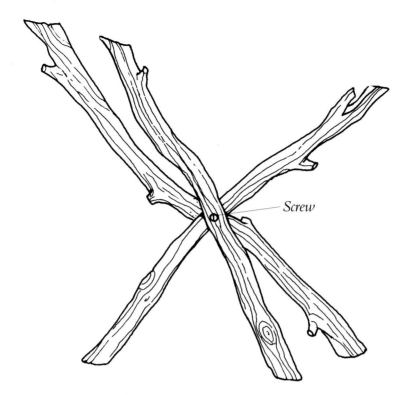

A. *View of Tripod from Side*

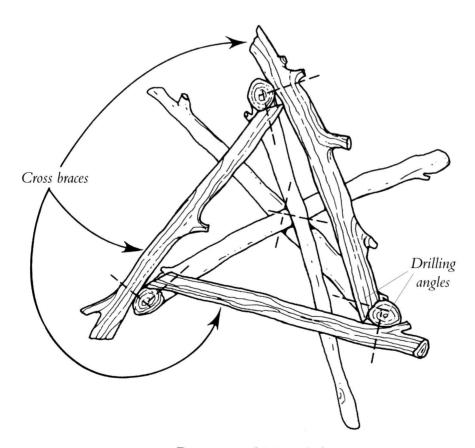

B. *View of Tripod from Top*

Birch Bark Box

Search the woods or the woodpile for fallen paper birch logs and collect scraps of bark to cover this small box. Flaws, scars, and rough spots in the bark will only make the final piece more interesting. The size of the scraps will determine the box's design. Very small pieces can be glued to the box in a patchwork to cover a larger surface. A plain, unfinished wooden box from a craft supply store or an old wooden cigar box forms the base. To cover the edges of the bark and to add decorative interest, the box shown is outlined with thin brown branches tacked on with decorative brass escutcheon pins.

SIZE

Box shown is 8½" wide × 5½" deep × 4" high

NATURE'S MATERIALS

Birch bark in sheets, strips, or scraps
¼"-diameter twigs with brown bark

SUPPLIES AND TOOLS

Wooden box
½" brass escutcheon pins
Wood glue
Drill and 1⁄16" drill bit
Tack hammer
Utility knife
Straightedge or ruler
White tacky glue
Damp cloth
Heavy book or weight to hold bark while glue sets

DIRECTIONS

1. Cut strips of bark to fit the sides of the wooden box, leaving about 1⁄16" clearance on all edges except at the joint between the lid and the base, where it should fit flush. Spread wood glue on one side of the box, position the bark, and weight it down with a heavy book or other weight. With a damp cloth wipe away any glue that squeezes out from under the bark. Allow the glue to set before repeating this procedure on the other sides of the box.

2. With the utility knife cut twigs to fit the edges of each side of the box and lid. Cut the ends of the twigs on the diagonal to form mitered joints at the corners. The vertical pieces on the sides of the box are cut straight.

3. With a thin bead of white tacky glue attach a twig to the box. Then drill through just the twig at one end and tack it down with an escutcheon pin. Repeat on the other end of the twig. Once the twig is attached to the box you can drill other holes evenly along the length of the twig and tap in the escutcheon pins. Repeat to attach other twigs.

4. Create a geometric pattern on the top of the box with short twigs using the same methods given above.

Birch Bark Wreath

Scraps of white birch bark from fallen trees or logs wrap a Styrofoam wreath form for a frontier-style wreath that couldn't be simpler to make. The stars are cut from the same bark (see Birch Bark Ornaments, below) but are reversed to show the brown underside. This is a good project for children to do under adult supervision.

SIZE

Wreath shown is 10" in diameter

NATURE'S MATERIALS

Scraps and strips of white birch bark: many about 2" × 8", larger and smaller as needed

SUPPLIES AND TOOLS

10"-diameter Styrofoam wreath form
Scissors
Low-temperature glue gun and glue stick
Pencil

DIRECTIONS

1. One at a time, wrap the pieces of bark around the wreath form and hot-glue them in place, holding each piece firmly until the glue sets. The low-temperature glue sets fast and requires that you work quickly to apply the bark to the form. Cover the entire wreath form with bark, overlapping the strips and using smaller pieces to fill in any gaps.

2. Draw stars on the back of the larger pieces of bark with a pencil and cut them out using sharp scissors. We made seven 2¼" stars, but you can make more smaller stars or fewer larger stars or mix sizes as desired. Peel off any loose, papery bark from the front and glue the stars to the wreath with the brown side facing out.

❀ *Birch Bark Ornaments* ❀

Here's a craft project that children will love. Draw simple shapes or images on the back of birch bark scraps with a pencil and cut them out with sharp scissors. The two paddlers in a canoe shown in the photo can hang on a Christmas tree, sit on a shelf, or serve as a bookmark. The stars glued to the wreath in the photo would make great Christmas ornaments. Just punch a hole in the top and attach string or floral wire for a hanger. That's all there is to it!

Wood Nymph Masks

An hour's walk in the brisk autumn air will turn up the materials to make one-of-a-kind exotic masks. Leaves and pine needles; pinecones, seeds, nuts, and pods; dried flowers, grasses, and berries; and a handful of bark with lichen can transform ordinary fabric masks into otherworldly creatures with the flick of a glue gun. The way the leaves are angled or the addition of whiskery pine needles can change expressions from gleeful to intense. If you want to make a stand to display your mask, see the Feather Mask project on page 93 for details.

SIZES

Face masks embellished as desired

NATURE'S MATERIALS

Matching pairs of any sturdy leaves, such as oak or beech

Grasses, bark, lichen, dried flowers, sheet moss, pine needles, pinecones, seeds, pods, nuts, or other woodland materials as desired

Thin branch or piece of bamboo for the handle, about 24" long

SUPPLIES AND TOOLS

Fabric face masks in woodsy colors (moss green, gray, tan, dusty yellow, rust, etc.)

Low-temperature glue gun and glue stick

Scissors

DIRECTIONS

1. Starting from the outside edge of the mask and working toward the nose, glue on background materials first, overlapping leaves, bark, or branches as you work. Arrange the materials to form a crest or peak at the top or to one side of the mask. Use matching leaves in pairs on either side of the mask or let the materials you have collected guide you as you go along. If leaves are not the right shape, trim them with scissors to fit. Glue finishing details on top. Be careful not to obscure the eyeholes or allow material to protrude into them.

2. Select a thin branch or piece of bamboo for a handle. Glue it to one side of the mask. When you're finished, carefully pick off the gossamer strands left by the glue gun.

Miniature Twig Furniture

Adirondack-style twig-and-branch furniture is all the rage with those who favor the rustic look, and in this diminutive size it is much easier to build. The settee, chairs, and tea table are made of black birch twigs, which are straight, slender, and flexible, with a pleasing, shiny bark. Scraps of bark shed from the sycamore tree form the settee seat and tabletop. While instructions given are for the furniture shown, we urge you to use the photo, instructions, and diagrams as guides to construct the basic forms and decorate as you please.

SIZES

As shown:

Chair is 2½" wide × 2¾" deep × 5" high

Settee is 7" wide × 3" deep × 5" high

Table is 3" wide × 2¾" deep × 3¼" high

NATURE'S MATERIALS

Black birch branches, ¼" and ⅛" in diameter at base and tapering to tips

Several small pieces of sycamore bark

SUPPLIES AND TOOLS

Pruning shears or wire cutters

Long-nosed pliers (helpful when gluing small twigs)

Utility knife

Brown acrylic paint

Small paintbrush

Hair blow-dryer

Ruler

Hot-glue gun and glue stick

DIRECTIONS

General

1. With pruning shears or wire cutters, clip the twigs. Then sort them into 3 piles: ¼"-diameter twigs, ⅛"-diameter twigs, and thin tips.

2. Lay the ruler on your work surface and use it to measure off and cut the twigs to the required lengths as shown in the cutting guide on page 75.

3. For the settee seat and the tabletop, cut the sycamore bark by scoring it with the utility knife and then snapping it along the scored line. Cut overlapping slabs so that when they are glued together they will form a rectangle 2½" × 4⅜" for the settee and 2½" × 3" for the tabletop. Make the settee seat and the tabletop by gluing together the overlapping slabs of bark.

4. Throughout the construction process allow the glue to harden between steps. When you are finished gluing a section, pick off as many of the gossamer hot-glue threads by hand as possible. Then blow off the rest with the hair dryer, being careful not to melt or weaken the joints.

5. If larger globs of glue are unsightly, touch them up with brown acrylic paint.

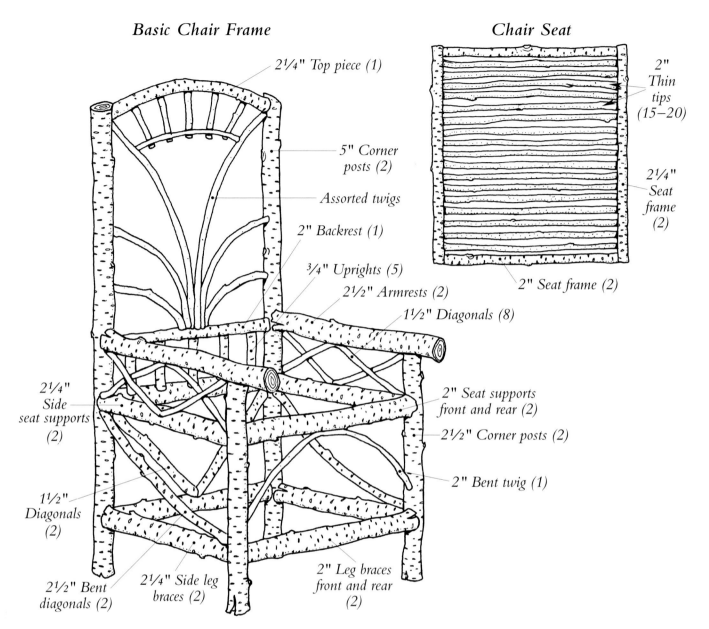

Basic Chair Frame

2¼" Top piece (1)

5" Corner posts (2)

Assorted twigs

2" Backrest (1)

¾" Uprights (5)

2½" Armrests (2)

1½" Diagonals (8)

2¼" Side seat supports (2)

2" Seat supports front and rear (2)

2½" Corner posts (2)

2" Bent twig (1)

1½" Diagonals (2)

2½" Bent diagonals (2)

2¼" Side leg braces (2)

2" Leg braces front and rear (2)

Chair Seat

2" Thin tips (15–20)

2¼" Seat frame (2)

2" Seat frame (2)

Chair

1. Hot-glue the 4 corner posts, the 4 seat supports, and the 4 leg braces together, following the diagram. While the hot glue is still warm and flexible, adjust the frame to make it level.

2. Glue on the 2 armrests, the backrest, the top piece for the back, and the 2 bent diagonals joining the front and rear corner posts.

3. Glue the 4 outer pieces of the seat frame together.

4. Be sure that the twigs that form the seat

are all cut so that they fit neatly inside the frame. Glue them in place, putting them as close together as possible.

5. Position the seat frame inside the chair and glue it to the support. (It is sufficient to glue it at each corner.)

6. Following the diagram, bend the thin tips for the chair back and glue them into position. Insert the five ⅛"-diameter uprights joining the backrest and the seat support; glue into place the 2"-long thin bent twig that joins the 2 front corner posts and adheres to the top of the seat support.

❋ *Twig Furniture Cutting Guide* ❋

All measurements are approximate. Trim as necessary to make the pieces fit.

Cut ¼"-diameter twigs:

Chair

2 corner posts: 5" long

2 corner posts: 2½" long

2 armrests: 2½" long

2 side leg braces, 2 side seat supports: 2¼" long

1 each front and rear leg braces and 1 each front and rear seat support pieces: 2" long

Settee

2 corner posts: 5" long

2 corner posts: 2½" long

2 armrests: 2½" long

2 side leg braces: 2¼" long

1 each front and rear leg braces; 1 each front and rear seat supports; and 1 seat backrest: 4½" long

3 vertical supports between front seat support and front leg brace: 1½" long

2 curved side pieces joining rear corner posts and top piece of the seat back: 3" long

Table

4 corner posts: 3" long

Cut ⅛"-diameter twigs:

Chair

1 backrest: 2" long

2 seat frame pieces: 2¼" long

2 seat frame pieces: 2" long

5 uprights joining backrest and seat support: ¾" long

2 bent diagonal pieces joining front and rear corner posts: 2½" long

2 diagonals joining top of rear seat support

to center of rear leg brace: 1½" long

1 bent top piece for back: 2¼" long

Settee

9 seat slats: 2¾" long

2 diagonals joining front and rear corner posts: 2¾" long

1 top piece for seat back: 7½" long

1 vertical center piece joining backrest to top piece of seat back: 2¾" long

4 diagonals for seat back: 1¾" long

2 diagonals for seat back: 3" long

4 diagonals between front leg brace and corner posts and between front leg brace and vertical supports: 1½" long

Table

2 each front and rear braces: 2½" long

1 center brace: 2½" long

4 side braces: 2¼" inches long

12 uprights to fit between top and bottom front, side, and rear braces: ½" long

Cut thin tips:

Chair

15–20 twigs to fill in seat frame: 2" long

8 twigs for diagonals joining seat supports and armrests: 1½" long

1 twig bent between front corner posts: 2" long

Twigs of various lengths for back

Table

4 twigs bent between corner posts: 4" long

2 twigs for front and rear of tabletop frame: 3" long

2 twigs for sides of tabletop frame: 2¾" long

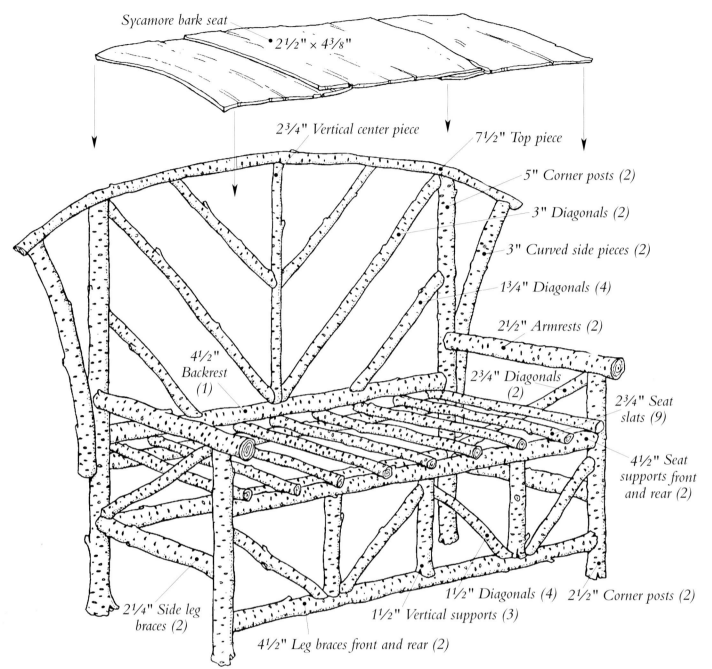

Sycamore bark seat

• 2½" × 4⅜"

2¾" *Vertical center piece*

7½" *Top piece*

5" *Corner posts (2)*

3" *Diagonals (2)*

3" *Curved side pieces (2)*

1¾" *Diagonals (4)*

2½" *Armrests (2)*

2¾" *Diagonals (2)*

2¾" *Seat slats (9)*

4½" *Seat supports front and rear (2)*

4½" *Backrest (1)*

2¼" *Side leg braces (2)*

4½" *Leg braces front and rear (2)*

1½" *Vertical supports (3)*

1½" *Diagonals (4)*

2½" *Corner posts (2)*

Basic Settee Frame and Seat

7. Glue into position the two 1½"-long ⅛" diagonals that join the rear seat support to the center of the rear leg brace.

8. Glue the 8 diagonal thin twigs that join the armrests and the seat supports.

Settee

1. Glue the 4 corner posts, the 2 seat supports, and the 4 leg braces together, as in step 1 of the chair directions and following the settee diagram.

2. Glue the seat slats to the seat supports, spacing them equally and allowing both fronts and backs of the slats to protrude over the seat supports.

3. Glue on the 2 armrests, the backrest (which should sit on top of the seat slats), and the 2 diagonals joining the front and rear corner posts.

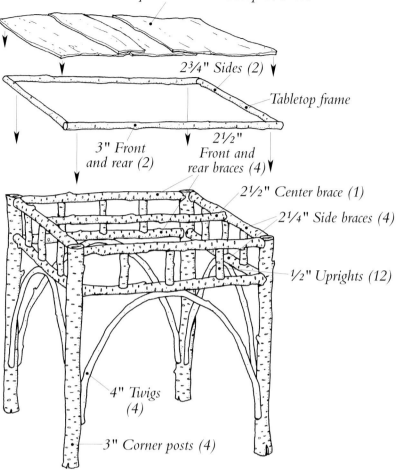

Sycamore bark tabletop 2½" × 3"

2¾" Sides (2)

Tabletop frame

3" Front and rear (2)

2½" Front and rear braces (4)

2½" Center brace (1)

2¼" Side braces (4)

½" Uprights (12)

4" Twigs (4)

3" Corner posts (4)

Basic Table Frame and Tabletop

4. Attach the bent top piece of the seat back to the rear corner posts and, while the glue is still warm, fit the vertical center piece securely between the backrest and the top piece. Hold the top piece against the rear corner posts and the vertical piece until the glue sets. Then position and glue the diagonals for the seat back and the two 3" curved side pieces as shown in the diagram.

5. Glue the 3 vertical supports between the front seat support and the leg brace. Position and glue the 4 diagonals between the front leg brace and the corner posts and between the front leg brace and the vertical supports, as shown in the diagram.

6. Glue the sycamore bark seat onto the seat slats.

Table

1. Glue the 4 corner posts, the 4 front and rear braces, and the 4 side braces together, as in step 1 of the chair directions.

2. Glue the 2½" center brace between the top side braces.

3. Insert and glue the twelve ½" uprights between the top and bottom front, rear, and side braces.

4. Bend and glue into position the 4 thin twigs between the corner posts and the bottom braces, as shown in the diagram.

5. Glue the 4 tabletop frame pieces to the top braces. Then glue on the bark tabletop as in the diagram and photo.

Spring and Fall Dolls

The two enchanting nature dolls seen on page 73 are dressed in their seasonal forest finery. The spring doll is as subtle as a shadow in her tea-dyed dress and curly moss hair. The fall doll is an autumn angel with velvet leaf-wings peeking from her back. A bit fragile for everyday play, the dolls are personalized craft pieces made for display. Devise a wooden stand like the one supporting the Feather Mask on page 94 or stage a tea party in a make-believe forest glade set with miniature twig furniture and china. Use the basic doll dress pattern and design your own outfits for the other seasons, perhaps a summer doll in a dotted swiss dress decorated with tiny dried flowers or a frothy white velvet snow queen with gossamer milkweed hair for winter.

SIZES

Dolls shown are 9" tall

NATURE'S MATERIALS

Green moss for hair

Acorns, dried star anise, or dried flowers for hair decorations

7" twig for arms of spring doll

18" piece of raffia or jute to tie and belt dress

Canella twig and pods (available from dried materials suppliers) or other decorative twig for spring dress

SUPPLIES AND TOOLS

Two 10" squares of muslin for each doll body

10" × 15" piece of linen, velvet, or other fabric for each dress

Matching thread

3 velvet leaves for fall dress

Polyester or cotton fiberfill

Embroidery hoop and needle

Embroidery floss: red and tan

Sewing machine   Iron

Straight pins

Tan sewing thread

2 cups of strong tea for dying fabric

White tacky glue

Tracing paper and pencil

DIRECTIONS

Doll Body

1. Soak the muslin in the tea for about 15 minutes. Let dry. Iron the fabric.

2. For each doll, transfer the pattern and facial features onto one piece of muslin (see Transferring Patterns, below).

❧ *Transferring Patterns* ❧

With a pencil, trace the doll body pattern and facial features from page 79 onto tracing paper. Note that the spring doll's arms end at about the elbow; they do not include the lower arms and hands. Tape the pattern tracing to a sunny window or light box; then center and tape a piece of muslin, wrong side up, over the pattern. Trace the body pattern onto the muslin. Turn the muslin right side up and align the muslin pattern outline with the tracing. Trace the facial features onto the muslin.

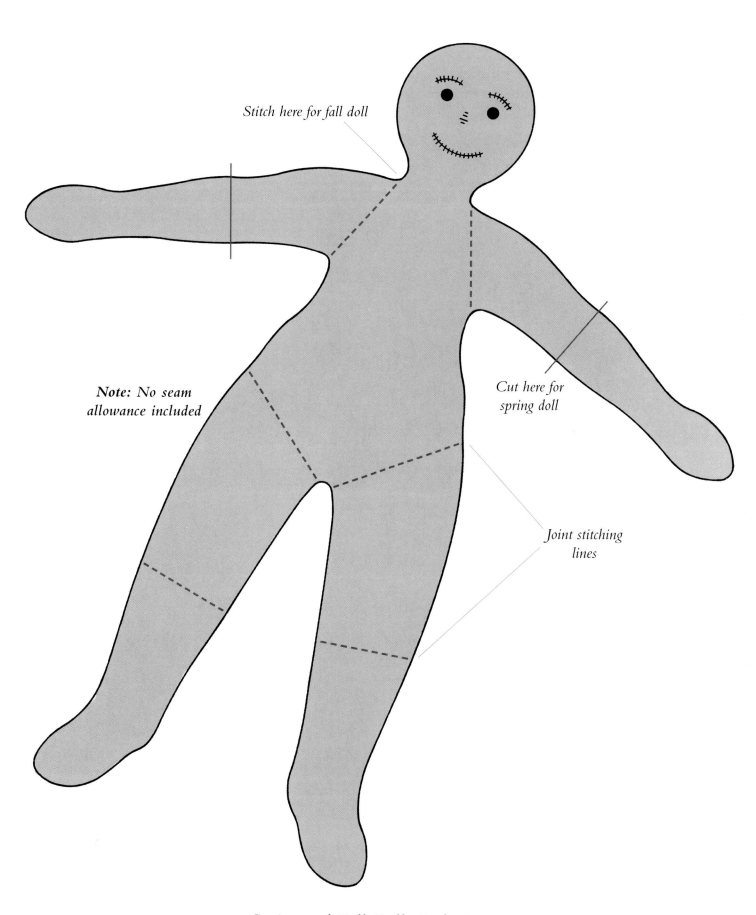

Stitch here for fall doll

Cut here for
spring doll

Joint stitching
lines

Note: *No seam
allowance included*

Spring and Fall Dolls Body Pattern

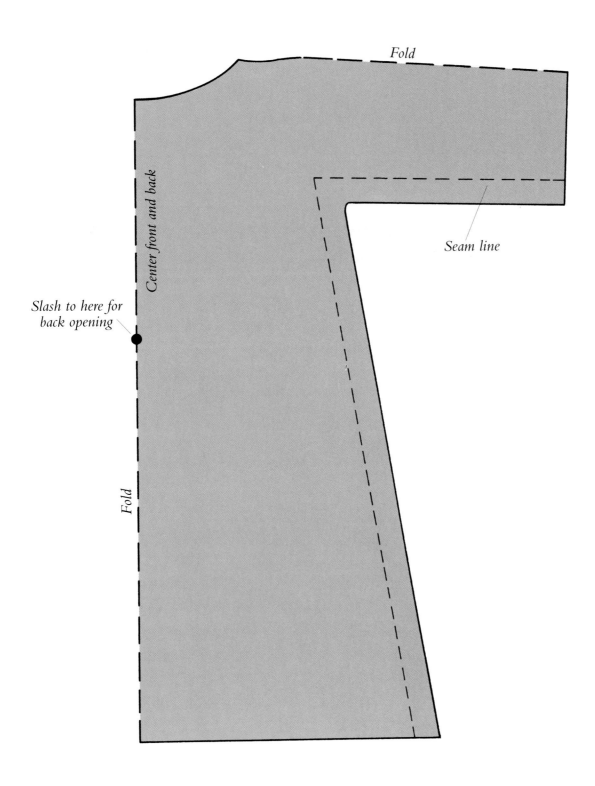

Fold

Center front and back

Seam line

Slash to here for
back opening

Fold

Spring and Fall Dolls Dress Pattern

3. Using an embroidery hoop to hold the fabric taut, embroider eyes, brows, nose, and mouth. The fall doll has tan French knots for eyes, a tan straight-stitch nose, and a red straight-stitch mouth. The spring doll's features are all in tan straight stitches.

4. Pin the muslin squares with right sides together. With the machine set for short stitches, sew along the marked line: For the spring doll leave the end of each arm open; for the fall doll sew along the entire marked outline. Trim the muslin to within ½" of the stitching line; clip curves. Cut a 2" slit through a single layer of fabric at the back of the body and turn the doll right side out through the slit.

5. Stuff the feet and legs lightly with fiberfill; machine-stitch along the lines at the hips and the knees through all thicknesses to form the joints. For the fall doll, stuff the arms and then stitch along the shoulder line. Stuff the head, neck, and torso. Whipstitch the turning slit closed. For the spring doll, insert the 7" twig through the arm openings and then whipstitch the fabric at the arm openings around the twig to secure it. Finish as for the fall doll.

6. (For best results, dress the doll before completing this step.) Glue the moss to the doll's head for hair. Glue a few small acorns, star anise, or dried flowers to the hair as desired.

Doll Dress

1. Trace the dress pattern onto tracing paper and cut it out. Fold the 10" × 15" fabric in half crosswise and then lengthwise. Pin the paper pattern to the folded fabric, matching the fold lines as indicated, and cut the dress out. Unfold the dress. Cut a slit for a center back opening as shown on the pattern.

2. With right sides together and a ¼" seam, sew the side and underarm seams. Turn the dress right side out. Fringe the lower edge or leave it raw.

3. Turn the fabric under along the neck edge and sew a line of gathering stitches around the neck, but do not knot or cut the thread. Slip the dress on the doll. Pull up the gathers to fit the neck, knot the thread, and clip the ends.

4. Repeat the gathering at the wrists of the fall dress; tie the wrists of the spring dress with raffia.

5. Finish the dresses. *Spring doll:* Wrap raffia around the waist, crisscrossing at the chest; secure with a few hand stitches and trim the ends of the raffia. Hand-sew a small canella twig or other dried material at the doll's waist. *Fall doll:* Glue a velvet leaf to the dress front. Twist the stems of 2 leaves together and hand-sew them to the back of the dress. Fan out the leaves like wings. Wrap the bodice of the dress with jute as for the spring doll.

❋ *Seasonal Fabrics* ❋

You can use a variety of fabric scraps for doll dresses that will evoke a particular season by their color and texture.

Spring: linen and cotton in neutrals and pastels

Summer: cotton lawn or batiste, dotted swiss, organdy, and eyelet in white

Autumn: velvet, burlap, fake suede, silk in deep gold, brown, green, burgundy, orange

Winter: velvet, fake fur, metallics, wool in snow-white and jewel tones

Thickets and Grasslands

Thickets flourish at the edges of woods, where increased sunlight encourages the dense growth of shrubs and vines. Honeysuckle, wild grapes, and Eurasian bittersweet can run rampant, choking out larger trees but providing protected nesting sites for birds and animals and a bounty of material for craft projects. Native grasses grow in open spaces, and if allowed to mature and seed themselves will produce a variety of feathery or podlike seed heads in many colors and textures. Moreover, grasses can be especially aromatic, and their fragrance will fill a room. When some Native Americans move into a new home, they tie bunches of sweet grass into a tight bundle, light it with a match, and allow the sweet smoke to waft throughout, to discourage evil spirits.

Bamboo is also from the grass family, but its rigid stalks can grow twelve feet tall and will spread into an impenetrable mass. Originally from the Orient, it can now be found in most temperate zones and will survive winters with temperatures below zero.

If you find a thicket with just the materials you need, contact the owners for permission to cut vines or bamboo. You may be doing them a favor.

Wild Grass Sheaf

A gathered and tied sheaf of grass standing on a side table is striking in its simplicity. Long taken for granted, wild grasses are being appreciated more of late. In rural meadows and along roadsides, grasses that have been routinely grazed or mowed are being allowed to grow and reestablish themselves, and suburban gardeners are giving cultivated stands of grass prominence in their borders and rock gardens. The time to harvest grasses is at the end of the growing season, when they have full heads of seed and have not yet been battered by winter winds. Some will be quite dry already; others will need to be spread out flat in a warm, dry attic for a few days. For instructions and information on drying plant materials, see Nature Crafts Basics.

SIZE

15"–24" tall, as desired

NATURE'S MATERIALS

Large handful of dried grass

About 15 strands of raffia 3' long

Assorted dried flowers (we used 3 wheat stalks, baby's breath, a rose, larkspur, strawflowers, and hydrangea)

SUPPLIES AND TOOLS

Fine floral wire

Wire cutters

Scissors

Hot-glue gun and glue stick

DIRECTIONS

1. Hold the grass with both hands, about ⅓ from the bottom. Turn your hands in opposite directions. The grass will begin to splay into a fan shape. Using the 15 strands of raffia together, wrap the raffia around the sheaf 2 or 3 times, tie the grass tightly, and make a bow. Trim the bottom of the grass with scissors so that the ends are even and the sheaf stands up straight. Trim the ends of the raffia.

2. Make a small bouquet of dried flowers. Wire them together at their bases and cut off the stems. Hot-glue the bouquet to the grass sheaf next to the bow.

3. Finish by gluing on a small bunch of dried hydrangea to hide the wire wrap on the bouquet.

Bittersweet Door Garland

There are two types of bittersweet vine: The American variety is rare and protected in some parts of the country, whereas the Eurasian bittersweet can be a pest, spreading its rust-red roots underground and wrapping itself around any upright plant it encounters. However, bittersweet is also very beautiful, especially in autumn, when its red, orange, and yellow berries are revealed after the leaves have fallen. If bittersweet is limited in your area, cut sparingly from any one plant to allow it to regenerate. For best results cut the branches before the yellow outer shells of the berries open and display them in a cool place. The graceful, asymmetrical garland shown here is pinned to the doorframe of a country cottage. Dried corn, shafts of wheat, and some pine and oak leaves are threaded through the vines. (Be advised that wild birds love the corn and wheat and will be at your door, knocking and devouring them as soon as they are discovered.) For instructions and information on drying plant materials see Nature Crafts Basics.

SIZE

As desired

NATURE'S MATERIALS

10–12 bittersweet vines, as long as possible

Wheat, bayberry, rose hips, leaves, and wild grasses

2 ears of dried field corn

SUPPLIES AND TOOLS

Wire brads

Floral wire

Pruning shears

Wire cutters

DIRECTIONS

1. Lay half of the vines on the ground. Lay the other half at a right angle to the first. Join the adjacent ends of the vines by wrapping them with wire.

2. Make wire loops and attach them to the back of the vines, one at the corner and one at the center along the top. If working on the ground is awkward, hang the vine at a convenient height to work on it comfortably.

3. Wire on more vines if the garland seems skimpy. At the corner, wire on 2 ears of dried corn and rose hips, wrapping the wire tightly so they won't fall off. The rest of the wild materials, grasses, and leaves may be woven in among the vines without wiring and among the wires to cover them. Hang the garland from small wire brads nailed into the top of the door trim, where they won't show.

Bittersweet Basket

The most common vines for making large free-form baskets are bittersweet and grapevine, or a combination of the two. The basket shown here is quite wild and woolly, with lots of smaller bittersweet vines with berries intertwined with grapevines in the basic basket form. You can make the basket complex or quite simple. Page 51 shows another version of this basket, made with large-diameter bittersweet vines and filled with dried maple leaf "roses." The density and thickness of the basket depend on its final use. The more vines you use, the sturdier the basket will be. Work with freshly cut vines, as they are more flexible and easier to weave.

SIZE

Basket shown is 24" long × 22" wide × 20" high

NATURE'S MATERIALS

Bittersweet and/or grapevine, approximately 6' long: 6 vines ½"–1" thick; 10 vines ¼"–½" thick

SUPPLIES AND TOOLS

Medium floral wire

Pruning shears and/or loppers

Wire cutters

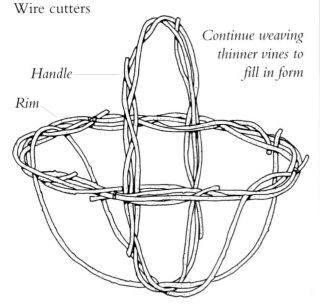

Handle

Rim

Continue weaving thinner vines to fill in form

Basic Form for Vine Basket

DIRECTIONS

1. Beginning with a thick vine, make a ring 2'–3' in diameter. Wrap the ends of the vine around the ring, securing them inside. If they will not stay, use a bit of floral wire to hold them in place. Wrap another vine around the first ring to make it sturdier and thicker. Tuck in the ends of the vine. Try to use as little wire as possible. This ring will form the rim of the basket.

2. Make a second ring a bit smaller than the first. This will form the handle. Insert the handle ring inside and perpendicular to the basket rim, as in the diagram. Wrap some more vines around the basket rim to hold the handle in place.

3. Wedge the end of 1 of the thinner vines between 2 larger vines in the basket rim. Make the vine dip and weave across the bottom of the handle to form the bottom of the basket. Bring it up and through the rim of the basket and back across the bottom. When you reach the end of the vine, tuck it in. Repeat with more vines. Be careful not to bend the vines too much, as they will break and become a weak point in the basket. As you are weaving, watch how the basket takes shape. Fill any gaps and weave thinner vines in and out to thicken and strengthen the basket.

Twig Swirl Wreath

Twig wreaths in this form are called swirl wreaths because of the angle of the branches. They can be made from a variety of twigs or wild grasses, or they can be purchased ready-made from craft suppliers and florists, as was the wreath pictured. The twig wreath is a graceful way to show off your best dried flowers. Design the color scheme to reflect the other colors in your home. This wreath combines the yellows of silica-dried black-eyed Susans with golden yarrow, and the coral shades of globe amaranth harmonize with a pale yellow wall and soft rose woodwork. For instructions and information on drying plant materials see Nature Crafts Basics.

SIZE

Wreath shown is 24" in diameter

NATURE'S MATERIALS

24"-diameter twig swirl wreath,
   or size desired
10 dried yarrow
10 dried globe amaranth
6 dried black-eyed Susans
6 pinecones, approximately 2" long
5 branches of dried lemon leaves

SUPPLIES AND TOOLS

Pruning shears
Hot-glue gun and glue stick

DIRECTIONS

1. Cut branches of lemon leaves about 8" long and arrange them around the wreath. Place them at the same angle as the swirled twigs and hot-glue them in place.

2. Leave 4"–5" stems on the yarrow and amaranth and hot-glue them onto the wreath with their stems oriented in the same direction as the swirled twigs.

3. Glue on the black-eyed Susans in any open spaces and finish with a few pinecones to fill out the design.

Twig Planter

Alacy twig planter is made of slender branches of the red-barked dogwood, a decorative shrub that usually grows about five feet tall and is prized for the rich red color of its young stems. Other plants, such as willows or American elder, will also provide a good supply of twigs for this and other craft projects if pruned to the base in early spring. This planter is not watertight, so add a plastic liner tray to hold potted plants.

SIZE

Basket shown is 8" wide × 21" long
 × 5" high

NATURE'S MATERIALS

8 branches about 2' long × ¼" in diameter,
 with side twigs left attached

6–8 branches 8"–10" long × ¼" in diameter

4 branches 5" long × ½" in diameter for
 corner posts

Sheet moss

Several plants in 4" plastic pots

SUPPLIES AND TOOLS

6½" × 20" piece of ¼"-thick plywood
 for base

Four #8 1" wood screws

1" panel nails

Barn-red exterior house paint or other color
 to coordinate with bark color

Paint primer/sealer

Plastic liner or tray to fit bottom of planter

Paintbrush

Drill and drill bit slightly smaller in diameter
 than wood screws

Hammer

Pruning shears

DIRECTIONS

1. Prime the plywood base on both sides and let dry. Paint it barn red and let dry.

2. To make the 4 corners, drill into the bottom ends of the 5" branches and through the 4 corners of the plywood base. Insert the screws from the underside of the base and screw them into the bottom of the branch posts.

3. With the hammer and 1" panel nails, tack the long branches to the posts to form the sides; tack the short branches to the posts across the ends. Leave long twigs attached to the branches and weave them into the sides.

4. Line the planter with pieces of sheet moss. Place a plastic tray in the bottom of the planter and then add plants still in their plastic pots. Tuck pieces of moss around the tops of the plastic pots to hide them.

Feather Mask

As a costume or an art form, a feather mask shows off one of nature's most beautiful and intricate creations. Feathers provide both maximum warmth for their weight and an astonishing range of patterns and colors. For centuries milliners and costumers relied on feathers from rare and exotic birds, many of which are now endangered. Today the main source of feathers is birds raised for food. Even fluffy marabou currently available is the down of a turkey or an ostrich and does not come from the stork, for which it is named. (Interestingly, ostrich feathers are clipped from live birds and will regrow.) Feathers from turkeys, ducks, pheasants, guinea hens, and ostriches are also dyed in a rainbow of colors and are sold packaged in craft supply stores.

SIZE

Face mask embellished as desired

NATURE'S MATERIALS

Feathers of choice; we used the following:

1 package of almond pheasant plumage natural feathers for the face

3 heart pheasant plumage natural feathers (black-tipped) for the plume

1 large marabou fluff feather for the plume

3 ostrich feathers (1 in each color: teal, brown, and eggshell) for the plume

3 white goose biots (long, slender feathers) for the plume

Thin branch or piece of bamboo for the handle, about 16" long × ¼" in diameter (optional)

1"-thick slice from a 6"-diameter log for a display base (optional)

SUPPLIES AND TOOLS

2 plastic face mask forms

Brown or gold elastic cord for wearing mask or wooden dowel 16" long × ¼" in diameter for mounting handle (as shown)

Fine floral wire

Drill and ¼" drill bit to attach handle to display base (optional)

Awl (or other tool to make holes in mask)

Wire cutters

Scissors

Tweezers

Hot-glue gun and glue stick

White tacky glue

DIRECTIONS

1. With scissors, round off the edges of both mask forms. Hot-glue 1 mask inside the other to make a stiffer form to work on. If you are planning to wear the mask rather than hold it by a handle, use the awl to punch holes in both sides of the mask form and tie on the elastic cord.

2. Spread a line of white tacky glue about 1" along the upper edge of the mask. Press the quill end of the almond pheasant feathers into the glue. Allow the other end to overlap the

edge of the mask. Continue along the top edge and around the sides, working 1" at a time. If the feathers are too long, cut off the bottom half and use just the decorative tips. Use tweezers to push the feathers into position. When the first row is complete, begin the second row, working in the same manner, starting at the top and overlapping the first row. Add more rows as necessary over the top of the mask. Be sure to overlap the feathers so that none of the plastic mask shows. Work around the bottom of the mask next. Then fan the feathers along the edges of the eyeholes, as shown in the photo, leaving the nose for last. Select the smallest feathers for the nose, cutting them down if necessary, and finish with 2 tiny feathers on the bridge of the nose.

3. To make the plume, bundle the 3 ostrich feathers and the marabou fluff together like a bouquet and wire the quill ends together. Position them in a graceful array and, with the glue gun, add the goose biots, the 3 heart pheasant feathers in a fan shape, and finally 3 almond pheasant feathers (use the photo as a guide). Hot-glue the plume inside the edge on one side of the mask.

4. If you want a handle on the mask, determine whether you wish to hold it in your right or left hand and hot-glue the branch, bamboo reed, or dowel to the corresponding inside edge of the mask.

5. To make a display stand, see Masks on Display, below.

❀ *Masks on Display* ❀

A beautifully crafted mask is a work of art worthy of display, either by itself or as part of a collection (see Wood Nymph Masks on page 71). To make a stand for your mask, hot-glue a wooden dowel, piece of bamboo, or twig approximately 16" long × ¼" in diameter to one inside edge of the completed mask. Drill a ¼" hole about ¾" deep in the center of a 1"-thick slab from a log 6" in diameter; do not drill all the way through the wood. Glue the dowel into the hole with white tacky glue.

Crocheted Raffia Baskets

The fiber of raffia palm leaves has long been used for tying up plants in gardens and lately has become especially popular for use in dried flower arrangements and as ties for gifts and floral bouquets. Since it is a soft fiber, it is not unpleasant to crochet and works up into soft, rather floppy baskets. In addition to its natural pale color, raffia is available dyed in many colors. The low, open basket has the added embellishment of a row of natural, bark-covered wooden beads sewn around the rim.

SIZES

As shown:

Low, open basket is 3½" high × 6" in diameter

Covered basket is 4½" high × 4" in diameter

Basket with handle is 6½" high (plus handle) × 6½" in diameter

NATURE'S MATERIALS

8-ounce bundles of raffia in the following colors: natural, dark green, light green, cranberry, rust

Small, cylindrical wooden beads with bark

2"–3" pieces of vine or twig for lid handle and to decorate large basket

SUPPLIES AND TOOLS

Crochet hooks, sizes I (5½ mm) and 15 (10 mm) or size for gauge

Beading needle

Nylon beading thread

Scissors

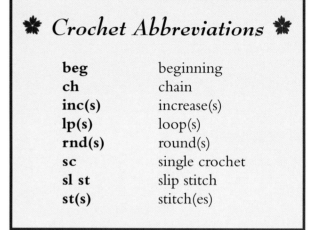

Crochet Abbreviations

beg	beginning
ch	chain
inc(s)	increase(s)
lp(s)	loop(s)
rnd(s)	round(s)
sc	single crochet
sl st	slip stitch
st(s)	stitch(es)

GAUGE

With smaller hook and single strand:
5 sc = 2"; 6 rnds = 2"

With larger hook and double strand:
3 sc = 2"; 4 rnds = 2"

DIRECTIONS

Low, Open Basket

(Note: Use smaller hook and single strand throughout.)

Beg at center bottom, with rust, ch 4, join with sl st to form a ring.

Rnd 1: Ch 1 (counts as first sc), 5 sc in ring, join with sl st to first sc—6 sc.

Rnd 2: Ch 1 (counts as first sc), sc in same st, 2 sc in next sc and in each sc, join—12 sc. Change to natural. *(Note: To change color, work last lp of last st with new color.)*

Rnd 3: Ch 1, *2 sc in next sc, sc in next sc; repeat from * around, join—18 sc.

Rnd 4: Ch 1, sc in next sc, *2 sc in next sc, sc in next 2 sc; repeat from * around, join—24 sc. Change to rust.

Rnd 5: Ch 1, sc in next 2 sc, *2 sc in next sc, sc in next 3 sc; repeat from * around, join—30 sc. Continue to inc in this manner, changing colors every other row, until 8 rnds have been completed.

Sides: Continuing in sc and changing colors as established, work even (without incs) until 18 rnds in all have been worked, ending with 2 rnds of rust. Do not fasten off.

Finishing: Continuing with rust, work 1 more rnd of sc. Fasten off. Weave in all ends.

Bead trim: Using beading needle and thread, string enough beads to fit around top edge. Sew beads in place with overcast stitching.

Covered Basket

(Note: Use smaller hook and single strand throughout.)

Beg at center bottom, with cranberry, ch 4, join with sl st to form a ring.

Rnd 1: Work as for Rnd 1 of low basket. Change to rust.

Rnd 2: Work as for Rnd 2 of low basket. Change to dark green.

Rnd 3: Work as for Rnd 3 of low basket.

Rnd 4: Continuing with dark green and working through back lps only *this rnd only*, work as for Rnd 4 of low basket. Change to light green.

Sides: Continuing in sc (resume working through both lps), work even (without incs), changing colors every rnd in established sequence, until 14 rnds in all have been completed, ending with cranberry; do not fasten off.

Last rnd: Continuing with cranberry, work 1 more rnd of sc. Fasten off.

Lid: Rnds 1–3: Work as for bottom of basket. Change to light green.

Rnd 4: Continuing to inc as before, work in sc. Change to cranberry.

Rnds 5 and 6: Work even; fasten off.

Finishing: Using 3 or 4 strands of cranberry, make a loop to hold decorative twig or vine handle and sew it to center top of lid. Place lid over top edge of basket and whipstitch edges together for about 2½". Weave in all ends. Insert handle into loop.

Large Basket with Handle

(Note: Use larger hook and double strand throughout, and work through back lps only.)

Beg at center bottom, with natural only, work as for Rnds 1–5 of low basket.

Rnd 6: Continuing with natural, work 1 more rnd, inc in same manner.

Rnds 7–14 (sides): Work even. At end of Rnd 14 change to dark green.

Rnds 15–16: Work even. Change to cranberry.

Rnd 17: Work even. Fasten off.

Handle: With natural, ch 6.

Row 1: Working through both lps, sc in 2nd ch from hook and in each ch across, ch 1, turn—5 sc.

Row 2: Sc (turning ch counts as first sc) in each sc across, ch 1, turn. Repeat Row 2 until handle measures 14" or desired length. Fasten off.

Finishing: With smaller hook and single strand of cranberry, sc along edge of handle all around. Fasten off. Sew ends of handle to opposite sides of basket at top edge. Weave in all ends. Wrap twig or piece of vine with raffia and attach to front center of basket by tying ends inside.

Bamboo Easels

Hardy bamboo, originally from China, is a member of the grass family and flourishes in milder climates, spreading its roots underground and forming an impenetrable grove seemingly overnight. (It has been known to take over gardens.) The stems taper from about 1½" in diameter at the ground and grow to be about 12' tall. Green when young and fresh, bamboo is easy to cut with loppers or pruning shears and is very strong. You can work with the bamboo while it's still green, but as it ages it will turn tan and become hard and inflexible.

These bamboo easels can be bound together with either flexible beading wire or strands of raffia. You can adjust the size to suit a particular framed print, photo, map, sampler, or mirror.

SIZES

Easels shown are 7" wide × 10" high;
    7" wide × 9" high; and 4" wide × 6" high

NATURE'S MATERIALS

3 stems of bamboo about 4' long × ½" in diameter at base tapering to ¼" at the top (Bamboo in larger diameters is sometimes available at craft stores, and smaller sizes are sold as garden stakes in garden centers.)

SUPPLIES AND TOOLS

20-gauge gold-finish beading wire or undyed raffia

Fine-toothed handsaw or backsaw

Drill and ¹⁄₁₆" drill bit

Wire cutters

Long-nosed pliers

Scissors

DIRECTIONS

1. Determine the size of the easel you want to make. The largest in the photo uses three 10" lengths of bamboo for the legs and one 7" length for the crosspiece. The back leg and the crosspiece are slightly larger in diameter than the front legs. Using a saw, cut the pieces for your easel.

2. Drill a hole 1" from the top of each leg and 2¼" from the bottom of each of the front legs. Drill a hole 1" from each end of the crosspiece. See diagram A on the next page for the position of the holes.

3. Cut an 18" piece of wire or raffia. Thread the strand through the holes at the tops of all 3 legs (see diagram A). Position the legs at the center of the strand. Wrap each half of the strand around an outside leg 4 times and twice between the legs and around the back leg. Knot the ends and cut off the excess. If you are using wire, tighten it gently with the pliers for a firm fit.

4. Cut another 18" length and thread it through the hole in 1 front leg and the hole in 1 end of the crosspiece (see diagram A). Wrap the wire or raffia tightly several times around the crosspiece and the front leg in the shape of an X and knot. Trim the ends.

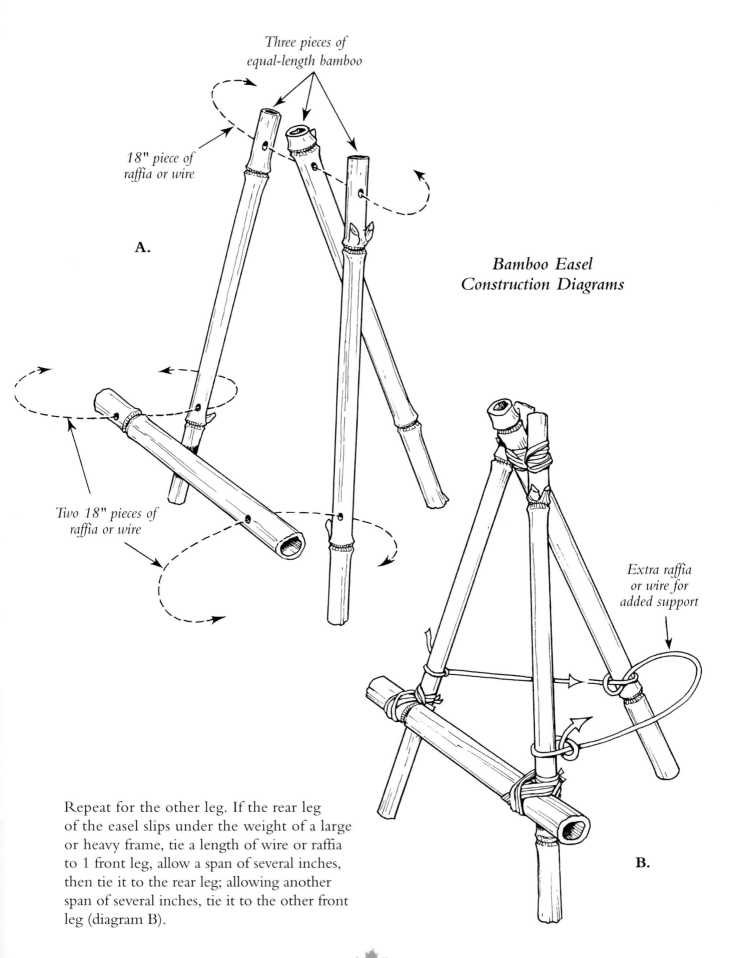

A.

Three pieces of
equal-length bamboo

18" piece of
raffia or wire

*Bamboo Easel
Construction Diagrams*

Two 18" pieces of
raffia or wire

Extra raffia
or wire for
added support

Repeat for the other leg. If the rear leg
of the easel slips under the weight of a large
or heavy frame, tie a length of wire or raffia
to 1 front leg, allow a span of several inches,
then tie it to the rear leg; allowing another
span of several inches, tie it to the other front
leg (diagram B).

B.

Door Spray

A door spray brings a bit of nature to an area you encounter frequently—the entrance to your home. This hardy spray was assembled in the early fall from plants found in the Northeast. (Some plants were bush-dried; others were picked green and dried as they hung.) It survived thirteen severe storms and continued to provide color and the pleasing scent of bayberry throughout the winter. Similar sprays can be made from plants native to any region. Many will lend themselves to a spray that brings both the color and the aroma of the out-of-doors.

SIZE

Determined by plants used

NATURE'S MATERIALS

Assorted wild and garden plants (we used silver artemisia, teasels, burrs, bayberry, green and silver santolina, rose hips, and bush-dried hydrangea)

SUPPLIES AND TOOLS

Floral wire

Green gardener's twine

Wire cutters

Scissors

DIRECTIONS

1. Gather the silver artemisia, teasels, burrs, and bayberry into a bundle and tie together with floral wire.

2. Insert the stems of the green and silver santolina under the wire.

3. Wrap green gardener's twine over the wire several times and tie securely, making a hanging loop.

4. Insert the wild rose hips and bush-dried hydrangea near the stem end, wrapping with more wire if necessary.

5. Hang the spray with the stem end up.

Walking Sticks

A hike can be anything from a stroll along a riverbank to a vigorous outing over more rugged terrain. Having a sturdy stick in hand is a big help when negotiating a steep slope, thick underbrush, or a slippery snowbank. Made from bamboo, maple, and hickory saplings, these walking sticks are strong as well as pleasing to the hand and eye. Find a downed sapling branch that's relatively straight, about 1" in diameter, and with some interesting detail if possible. The stained stick shown has a twisted indentation near the top, the result of a choking vine that caused it to grow in a spiral shape. A bittersweet vine entwined around a small maple was left intact, spiraling the length of the stick. If a sapling's bark is smooth and comfortable, leave it on, or remove only enough of the bark to make the handle. Varnish is optional, depending on the desired look.

SIZE

As shown:

Bamboo stick is 55" long

Twisted vine stick is 42" long

Stained hickory stick is 45" long

NATURE'S MATERIALS

Bamboo, hickory, maple, or other sturdy sapling or branch

3–5 lengths of rawhide for strap, ⅛" wide × 30" long or as desired (3 were used for the bamboo stick; the remaining sticks used 1 each)

SUPPLIES AND TOOLS

Loppers for cutting branches or saplings

Fine-toothed handsaw

Drill and ¼" drill bit

Sandpaper

Scissors

Optional

Metal chair leg tip or glide

1½" length of 1"-diameter brass pipe

Wood stain

Varnish, semigloss finish

1" chisel to remove bark

Utility knife

Hammer

Paintbrush

DIRECTIONS

Bamboo Walking Stick

Saw each end of the bamboo, just beyond the natural joint, to the desired length. (Using the handsaw rather than the loppers prevents the bamboo from splitting.) Drill a ¼" hole 1½" from the top all the way through the bamboo. Braid 3 lengths of rawhide together, thread the ends through the hole, and knot them together. Trim the ends with scissors.

Wooden Walking Sticks

Cut the branches or saplings to length with the saw. Peel off the bark if you like, using a chisel and a utility knife. Sand rough spots smooth. Drill a ¼" hole for the strap. Stain and/or varnish the stick if desired. Thread a length of rawhide through the hole, knot the ends, and trim them with scissors.

Option: Whittle the bottom end of the stick and slip on the piece of brass pipe. The fit should be tight. Tap the pipe with a hammer until it extends about ½" below the end of the stick. Insert the metal chair tip into the end of the pipe and tap it into place.

Twig Boats

Interesting fragments of bark, driftwood, twigs, and leaves take on amazing character when made into a collection of tiny boats—a sort of rickety regatta. Seaworthiness is not required, but should the boats actually float upright, you could stage a race in the local brook. The first one to drift over the finish line—or even get to it—would be the winner.

SIZE

Boats shown are approximately 6" long

NATURE'S MATERIALS

Branches, twigs, bark, leaves, grasses

SUPPLIES AND TOOLS

Drill and drill bits in assorted sizes
Utility knife

DIRECTIONS

1. Choose a broken branch or piece of driftwood that most resembles the hull of a boat. Use the utility knife to shape the wood, always carving away from your body and your other hand.

2. Cut a twig to use as a mast. Drill or gouge a hole in the center of the boat to hold the mast. Whittle the end of the mast to fit the hole tightly. Insert the mast into the hole.

3. Make a sail from a leaf or a piece of bark. Make slits in the sail and slip it on over the mast.

By experimenting with the center of gravity and with wider pieces of wood for the hull, you may arrive at a design that works.

Streams and Marshes

Mucking about in a stream in early spring is every child's passion. As an adult you may experience the same fascination. Pebbles and rocks washed by cold, fresh water seem to have brighter colors, revealing striated veins of yellow, pink, or white quartz or sparkling flecks of mica.

As a stream cuts into the soil forming its banks, it reveals many layers of earth. Beneath topsoil black with humus may be reddish or gray strands of clay. Newly green mosses flourish along the banks—some spiky, others like velvet. Ferns of all sizes unfurl their heads and open into elegant sprays.

Willows grow along the edges of brooks, providing slim branches for basket weaving and furniture. Their roots hold the banks together and thus both prevent erosion and keep the stream in its course. A leisurely outing along a stream may inspire you to make the projects in this chapter or to think of others. Wear rubber boots when you go forth, and try not to step on the skunk cabbage; it really deserves its name.

Clay Bead Jewelry

Natural clay deposits can sometimes be found at the edge of a dirt road or stream or wherever a cut through the earth reveals different strata. Often large veins of clay exist near the site of an old brick works. In its pure state, without sand or other soils mixed in, clay soil is very sticky, can be molded, and hardens as it dries. Colors range from rusty red to gray and even white. Of course, the easiest way to obtain clay is from a craft supplier. The clay beads used in the jewelry pictured were made with self-hardening clay, which does not require any baking. Clay is also available in a wide range of colors that can be hardened in your home oven. Making beads is simple; in fact, jewelry making can be enjoyed by the whole family. Look for "antique" metallic beads and jewelry findings, such as earring wires and T-pins, at a craft supplier.

SIZES

As shown:

Earrings are 2½" long

Gray bead and silver heart necklace is 33" long

Marbled bead necklace is 30" long

Coiled bracelet is adjustable

NATURE'S MATERIALS

Self-hardening gray clay

Self-hardening red clay

SUPPLIES AND TOOLS

Coiled bracelet wire

Pierced ear wires or nonpierced earring backs

T-pins

Nylon beading cord and beading needle

12"-long wood skewers

Clear glossy acrylic spray

Clear nail polish

Round-nosed pliers (to make loops)

Flat-nosed pliers (to close loops)

Wire cutters

Scissors

Beads

Earrings

2 silver tear-shaped beads

4 silver rosebud beads, 6 mm

Gray Bead and Silver Heart Necklace

15 decorative silver beads (14 in matching pairs, 1 for top of necklace)

42 silver rosebud beads, 6 mm

6 plain brushed-silver pony beads

1 silver heart-shaped bead

Marbled Bead Necklace

10 large copper pony beads

20 small copper pony beads

5 large brushed-silver pony beads

20 silver rosebud beads, 6 mm

Bracelet

8 small decorative silver beads

5 large copper pony beads

26 small cylindrical plain copper pony beads

2 copper pony beads, 6 mm

❧ *Making Beads* ❧

From a large piece of clay pull off a section and roll it between your hands to form a bead ¾" in diameter or whatever size is desired. While you are working, keep the large piece of clay wrapped in plastic wrap or a plastic bag so it will not dry out. To make the hole in the bead, insert a skewer into one side and push it just beyond the center. Remove the skewer and poke it into the bead from the other side to complete the hole. Working from both sides will keep the bead's round shape. When you have completed all the beads, thread them gently onto skewers, leaving space between them and being careful not to deform the shape. Suspend the skewers from the rim of a bowl or pot and let the beads dry thoroughly.

Lightly spray the beads, still on the skewers, with acrylic sealer. Suspend them again to dry and repeat the process until you have an even, glossy surface.

To make marbled beads: On a smooth surface, roll out a long snake of clay, about ¼" in diameter, in each of 2 chosen colors. Twist the 2 snakes together loosely. Cut off a ¾" piece of the twist and roll it into a round bead. As you roll the bead the 2 colors will blend to become marbled. Make the hole, let dry, and spray as described above.

DIRECTIONS

Earrings

Make 2 red clay beads approximately ¾" in diameter, following the directions for making beads, above. Using the diagram as a guide, insert a T-pin through a silver tear-shaped bead. Trim the end of the T-pin about ¼" from the top of the bead. Using the round-nosed pliers, bend the end of the pin into a loop. Clip off the

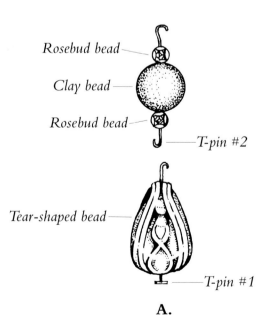

Rosebud bead —

Clay bead —

Rosebud bead —

— T-pin #2

Tear-shaped bead —

— T-pin #1

A.

— Ear wire

B.

Earring Construction

T end of another T-pin and make an open loop. Hook it onto the loop made on the tear-shaped bead and close the loop with the flat-nosed pliers. Thread a 6-mm silver rosebud bead, a red clay bead, then another rosebud bead onto the straight end of this T-pin. Bend the straight end into a loop and hook it onto the ear wire. Close the loop.

Gray Bead and Silver Heart Necklace

1. Make 20 gray clay beads approximately ¾" in diameter, following the directions in the Making Beads box.

2. Using the diagram below as a guide, insert a T-pin through the bottom of the heart-shaped bead. Trim the end of the T-pin about ¼" from the top of the bead. Using the round-nosed pliers, bend the end of the pin into a loop. Cut a ½" piece of T-pin to make another loop and hook it through the first loop; close it with the flat-nosed pliers.

3. With the photo as a guide, use doubled nylon beading cord and the beading needle to string the beads with the heart and larger silver beads at the center of the necklace, the smaller ones near the top, and a rosebud bead on either side of each clay and silver bead.

Loop

Loop

Heart

T-pin

Gray Bead and Silver Heart Necklace Construction

When you're finished, tie a tight square knot, cut the ends, and dab the knot with clear nail polish. Move the center top bead over the knot to cover it.

Marbled Bead Necklace

Make 20 marbled beads and 5 gray beads, all approximately ½" in diameter, following the directions for making beads, on the facing page. Using doubled nylon beading cord and the beading needle, and with the photo as a guide, string the beads, with 1 gray bead following 4 marbled beads, with sets of smaller beads in between. Finish off as explained in step 3 of the gray bead necklace.

Bracelet

1. Make 8 red clay beads and 4 gray clay beads, approximately ¾" in diameter, following the directions for making beads, on the facing page.

2. Using the flat-nosed pliers, bend a closed loop at one end of the coiled wire. Thread a 6-mm copper pony bead onto a T-pin. Trim the end of the T-pin about ¼" from the top of the bead and use the round-nosed pliers to bend it into a loop. Repeat with another 6-mm copper pony bead. Hook the loop of one of the 6-mm beads into the end of the coiled wire and bend the loop closed with the flat-nosed pliers.

3. With the photo as a guide, thread the beads onto the coiled wire, separating every large clay bead with sets of 3 smaller beads. End the bracelet with the second 6-mm copper bead. Trim the end of the coiled wire, make a loop, hook it through the bead loop, and bend it closed.

Moss-Covered Flowerpot

It looks like a product of nature, but this decorative planter is actually a plain clay flowerpot that was easily transformed with the addition of sheet moss, dried leaves, and berries. Raffia strands give the semblance of wrapping but are really just for looks. A potted flowering plant slipped into the moss pot will make repotting or changing the plant simple. For instructions and information on drying plant materials see Nature Crafts Basics.

SIZE

Determined by size of flowerpot

NATURE'S MATERIALS

Sheet moss
Raffia
Dried pepper berries
Dried lemon leaves

SUPPLIES AND TOOLS

Clay or plastic flowerpot of choice
Scissors
Hot-glue gun and glue stick

DIRECTIONS

1. Using hot glue, cover the flowerpot with sheet moss a section at a time. Along the top edge of the pot, wrap moss to the inside and glue it in place.

2. Cut 12" strands of raffia. Glue one end inside the top of the pot. When the glue is set, pull the other end to the bottom of the pot and glue in place. Repeat with several strands running at different angles.

3. Glue a cluster of pepper berries and lemon leaves to the side of the pot.

Moss Wreath

Small clusters of three different wild mosses embellish the store-bought sheet moss that covers this wreath form. The wonderful moss textures and colors, from pale dusty green to deep emerald, provide a verdant background without using too much wild plant material. The moss fragments are tied to the wreath form with raffia and highlighted with dried red rosebuds, galax leaves, rose hips, acorns, and tiny hemlock cones. Sheet moss makes a natural canvas that can be decorated with all sorts of dried flowers, leaves, nuts, pods, and lichen. Fill your collecting basket with whatever is available and let your imagination lead the way. For instructions and information on drying plant materials see Nature Crafts Basics.

SIZE

Wreath shown is 12" in diameter

NATURE'S MATERIALS

Sheet moss

5 clumps of wild moss

Raffia

Dried rosebuds

Dried galax leaves

Acorns

Rose hips

Hemlock cones

SUPPLIES AND TOOLS

12"-diameter Styrofoam wreath form

Floral wire

Wire cutters

Hot-glue gun and glue stick

DIRECTIONS

1. Make a loop of floral wire for a hanger and wire it to the wreath form.

2. Using hot glue, cover the wreath form with sheet moss a section at a time, leaving open spaces for wild moss. Glue clumps of wild moss in position and wrap them with raffia.

3. Using the photos as guides, glue on clusters of rosebuds and surround them with galax leaves. Add acorns, rose hips, and tiny hemlock cones, tucking them between the clusters of flowers.

4. Slip several strands of raffia through the wire loop and knot them to form a hanger.

Driftwood-and-Sand Frame

The well-worn quality of weathered wood or driftwood is a fitting accent for a frame housing a favorite old sepia-toned family photograph. Sand was used to create a backdrop for the wood, but gravel, pebbles, or moss collected near a streambed can be added to a frame with extraordinary results. This ready-made frame came with a corrugated cardboard filler, which became the textured mat for the photo.

SIZE

Frame shown is 10" × 12"

NATURE'S MATERIALS

5–6 pieces of weathered wood or driftwood

Sand, fine gravel, or tiny pebbles

SUPPLIES AND TOOLS

Ready-made wooden picture frame with a
    flat surface on the front

Finishing nails: 1" and 1½", depending on
    thickness of wood pieces

Acrylic paint: black and white

Paintbrush

Small brush for glue

Handsaw to cut wood

Drill and drill bit slightly smaller in diameter
    than nails

Hammer

White tacky glue

Newspaper

DIRECTIONS

1. Cover the work surface with newspaper. Dip the brush first in one color and then in the other before brushing the paint on the frame. Paint the frame with a mixture of black and white paint to create streaky shades of gray. Let dry.

2. Brush a generous amount of glue on the flat surface of the front of the frame. While it is still wet, sprinkle sand on to cover all the glue. Let dry and shake off the excess sand.

3. Arrange the pieces of wood on the frame, cutting them to size if necessary. Drill through the wood and into the frame and nail the wood in place, using nails of appropriate sizes.

Southwest Sand Garden

The warm, dry environment of a winter living room with central heating will make these cacti feel right at home in their miniature sand garden. Sand from a brook or beach forms the landscape. If sand from an ocean beach is used, it must be rinsed thoroughly to remove the salt. Bark, an antler, seedpods, and pieces of craggy pink granite and water-worn brick complete the desert scene, but feel free to use whatever artifacts of nature are available to you.

SIZE

Box shown is 15" long × 9¾" wide × 2" deep

NATURE'S MATERIALS

3 small cacti

Potting soil

Sand

Antler or weathered branch

Bark

Stones

Seedpods

SUPPLIES AND TOOLS

Rough-sawn ⅜"-thick wood, such as
    plaster lath: 2 pieces 15" long × 2" wide;
    2 pieces 9" long × 2" wide

9" × 14¼" piece of ¼"-thick plywood

8½" × 14" piece of 1"-thick Styrofoam

1" wire brads

Tan acrylic paint

7"- or 8"-diameter plastic plant saucer

Wood glue

Paintbrush

Hammer

DIRECTIONS

1. Using the hammer and wire brads, nail the shorter pieces of wood to the inside of the long pieces to make the frame of the box.

2. Put the frame of the box on the work surface. Spread wood glue around all 4 inside bottom edges of the box, lay the plywood in the frame, and nail it in place from the outside, placing the wire brads ⅛" up from the bottom of the box. The glue will prevent the sand from leaking out from the bottom of the box. Let dry thoroughly.

3. Paint the exterior of the box with acrylic paint. Let dry thoroughly.

4. Cut a hole in the Styrofoam to hold the plastic saucer. Spread some glue on the bottom of the box and insert the Styrofoam into the box. Let the glue dry.

5. Arrange the cacti in the plant saucer and surround them with some potting soil. Place the saucer in the hole in the Styrofoam and fill the box with sand, covering the saucer. Add the decorative elements in a pleasing arrangement. The sand can be sprinkled lightly with water to get a crinkly texture. (*Note:* When watering the cacti, pour the water only in the area of the saucer.)

Pressed Ferns

The many types and shapes of ferns are beautiful when pressed. The fronds can be bent slightly into graceful curves, and a grouping of several varieties—such as maidenhair, Boston, and lady fern—looks very dramatic when mounted on Japanese rice paper or textured mulberry paper, which contains flecks of bark and leaves. The smaller of the frames pictured also contains dried sage leaves and a bit of privet. Look for ferns with interesting textures, shapes, and colors along roadsides and streambeds and in marshy areas. Many people grow ferns in the shady areas of their gardens. For instructions and information on pressing plant materials see Nature Crafts Basics.

SIZES

As shown:

Large frame is 16" × 20"

Small frame is 9½" × 12"

NATURE'S MATERIALS

Assorted pressed ferns and other leaves

SUPPLIES AND TOOLS

Ready-made picture frames (the large one in the photo is black plastic; the smaller is a piece of glass clamped to hardboard with metal clips)

Rice or mulberry paper the same size as the frame (from an art supply store)

Glass cleaner

Paper towels

DIRECTIONS

1. Disassemble the frame and clean the glass on both sides. Rinse with clear water and dry.

2. Lay the paper on the frame backing and place the pressed fronds and leaves on top.

3. Place the glass over the fronds and leaves. Holding the glass and backing firmly so the leaves do not slip, reassemble the frame.

Stone Herb Markers

Smooth, rounded stones washed by flowing water for millennia make handsome plant markers. Stones clearly painted with labels bearing the common or Latin botanical names of your plants will identify the herbs or flowers in your garden. You can also paint a large rock with your family's name and place it at the end of the driveway or the path to your door. A wonderful project for children is to paint stones with their own designs and give them as gifts that can be used as paperweights or, with a piece of adhesive felt on the bottom, placed on display.

SIZES

Markers shown are 4"–6" wide

NATURE'S MATERIALS

Smooth, round stones from stream, brook, or beach

SUPPLIES AND TOOLS

Acrylic paint: off-white, dark green, and dark brown

Wide (½"–¾") paintbrush

Thin paintbrush for lettering

Sponge

Pencil

DIRECTIONS

1. With pencil, lightly draw an oval on the stone.

2. Using the wide brush, paint inside the oval with off-white paint. Let dry thoroughly and repeat with another coat for even coverage. Let that dry thoroughly.

3. With pencil, lightly write the herb or plant name in the center of the oval. If you are not pleased with the placement of the letters, use a damp sponge to wipe off the pencil marks and try again.

4. With the thin paintbrush and green paint, paint the herb name.

5. Using green paint and green mixed with off-white, paint decorative borders of leaves as shown in the photo. Let dry thoroughly.

6. Add water to a tiny amount of brown paint to make it very transparent. Dip a sponge in it and lightly dab on the painted area of the stone to give it a soft, antique look.

Sunprint Sachets

S unprint projects are fun for both children and adults. The printing is made easy with specially treated cotton squares, which are sold in quilt, craft, and fabric stores or by mail order; instructions are included with the fabric. Sewing these sunprint sachets couldn't be simpler, whether made by hand or by machine. Our natural environment offers up a host of materials that can be used to make sunprints. Follow your creative impulses and improvise to suit your design. For instructions and information on drying plant materials see Nature Crafts Basics.

SIZES

Sachets as shown:

Bordered pillows are 9½" square and 9" wide × 7" high

Button pillow is 8" wide × 5¾" high

Tied sachets are 7½" wide × 7¾" high (unhemmed)

NATURE'S MATERIALS

Twigs, flowers, leaves, grasses, nuts, branches of evergreen, sprigs of herbs for sunprints and to tie onto sachets

Dried balsam, lavender, or other scented herbs for filling sachets

1 yard of raffia

SUPPLIES AND TOOLS

Sunprint fabric in 8" squares

Small print or solid cotton fabrics for pillow sachet borders and backings

Polyester fiber filling

Assorted buttons as trim for button pillow sachet

Sewing thread to match fabric

Sewing thread in contrasting color for button pillow sachet

Needle

Sewing machine (optional)

Scissors

Iron

DIRECTIONS

1. Using twigs, leaves, flowers, grasses, and so on, make sunprints, following the manufacturer's directions that come with the sunprint fabric. Improvisation is encouraged.

2. See the Sunprint Cutting Guide for the fabric requirements for each sachet.

❦ *Sunprint Cutting Guide* ❦

For 9½" square pillow sachet
  Cut 4 strips of border fabric: 2 each
    1¾" × 8", 2 each 1¾" × 11"
  Cut backing fabric: 11" square
  Sunprint: 8" square

For 9" × 7" pillow sachet
  Cut 4 strips of border fabric: 2 each
    1¾" × 5½", 2 each 1¾" × 10"
  Cut backing fabric: 8" × 10"

Trim sunprint to 5½" × 7½"

For tied sachets
  Cut backing fabric: 8" square
  Sunprint: 8" square

For button-trimmed pillow sachet
  Cut 2 strips of border fabric: 1¾" × 8"
  Cut backing fabric: 8½" × 8"
  Trim sunprint to 6½" × 8"

Bordered Pillows

1. With right sides together and ½" seams, stitch the shorter border strips to opposite sides of the sunprint. In the same manner, stitch the long strips to the top and bottom of the sunprint and its side borders.

2. With right sides together and ½" seams, stitch the pillow front to the backing, leaving an opening for turning. Turn to the right side and press. Stuff with fiberfill and balsam. Slipstitch the opening closed.

Tied Sachets

1. With right sides together and ¼" seams, stitch sunprint to backing fabric along 3 sides. Make a narrow hem on the top edge or leave it raw. Turn to the right side and press. Stuff with fiberfill and dried lavender until about three-quarters full.

2. Tie the sachet with a double length of raffia and tuck a sprig of decorative leaves, herbs, or nuts into the knot.

Button-Trimmed Pillow

1. The side edges of the border and the backing are left unhemmed. Unravel along one long side of each border strip to make a ¼" frayed edge. With ¼" seams and right sides together, stitch the nonfrayed edge of a border strip to each long side of the sunprint. Press seams open.

2. Along the top edge of the pillow front, turn a 1" hem to the wrong side, turn again, and stitch along the fold. Repeat with the backing piece, hemming along one of the 8½" edges.

3. With right sides together and a ¼" seam, stitch the pillow front and backing along the bottom, unhemmed edge. Turn and press. With wrong sides together, topstitch the side seams just inside the frayed edge. Stuff the sachet with fiberfill and dried herbs.

4. Thread the needle with contrasting-color thread and sew buttons along the top edge of the pillow through all thicknesses to close it.

Crystal Jewelry

Depending on the geology of a region, it is possible to walk down a country road or along a streambed and see bits of quartz crystals or other mineral chips in their original crystalline shapes, with facets that reflect the light and make them sparkle. Other jewels of nature will be found as softly rounded pieces that have been tumbled by the action of a river or sea. Smooth, rounded stones can be brought to a high polish by tumbling them further in a rotating canister filled with water and sand or polishing compounds. Fortunately, you don't have to leave it to luck to find these mineral fragments. Minerals (and books to identify them) are available by mail, through craft and jewelry maker suppliers, or as rock collections. Flexible craft wire makes easy work of wrapping the stones, and inexpensive chain necklaces, bracelets, and plain barrette backs provide the basics for making your own collection of gemstone jewelry.

SIZES

As shown:

Necklace is 30" long

Pendant is 22" long

Bracelet is 8" long

Barrette is 3½" long

NATURE'S MATERIALS

For all jewelry shown

18 assorted mineral stones (we used 3 clear quartz, 8 rose quartz, 4 silvery hematite, 2 amethyst, and 1 pyrite crystal)

SUPPLIES AND TOOLS

20-gauge silver-colored craft wire

22-gauge craft wire: 1 spool each of gold-colored and silver-colored

5 silver jumprings for bracelet

8" linked-chain bracelet

30" linked-chain necklace

Metal barrette back

1 yard perle cotton (shown), satin, or leather cord for pendant

Round-nosed pliers (to make loops)

Flat-nosed pliers (to close loops)

Wire cutters

Hot-glue gun and glue stick

❋ **Wrapping Stones** ❋

Using the photo as a guide, wrap tumbled or faceted stones individually with 20-gauge silver wire the same way you would wrap a package, twisting the wire where it crosses, to hold the stone tightly.

DIRECTIONS

Necklace

1. Wrap each of 6 rose quartz and 1 clear quartz stones following the instructions in the box above, leaving an extra 3" of wire on each stone.

2. Wire the stone directly to the necklace chain at even intervals: Insert the wire through the chain link and wrap the end of the wire several times around the base of the loop to secure it.

Pendant

1. Select a faceted piece of crystal with a pointed end. Wrap the stone following the instructions in the box on page 127. Before cutting off the wire, make a loop and twist the wire around the base of the loop several times. Cut the wire and use the flat-nosed pliers to tuck the end around to the back.

2. Knot the ends of the cord. Using the diagram as a guide, slip the pendant on the doubled cord, loop the cord back over the knot, and pull down on the pendant so it is centered at the bottom of the loop.

Bracelet

1. Wrap 4 tumbled hematite stones and a pyrite crystal following the instructions in the box on page 127. Before cutting each stone's wire, use the round-nosed pliers to make a loop at the end; then twist the wire around the base of the loop several times to secure it.

2. Hook each stone to a jumpring and attach the rings at even intervals to the chain bracelet. Close the jumprings securely with the flat-nosed pliers.

Barrette

1. Using a strand of 22-gauge gold wire and a strand of 22-gauge silver wire together, as a double strand, wrap 2 amethysts, 2 rose quartz, and 1 clear quartz following the instructions in the box on page 127. Cut the ends of the wire with wire cutters.

2. Try out the placement of stones on the barrette back. When you are satisfied, hot-glue them to the barrette.

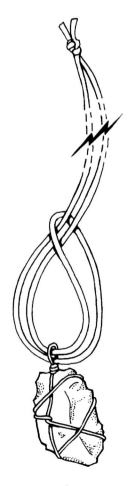

A.

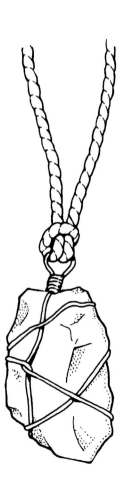

B.

Crystal Pendant Necklace

The Seashore

Summer vacations often lead to a beach. We have all collected souvenirs to remind us of the change of pace. Summer memories are different from the routine as well: views of waves and the distant horizon, images of the shining sand inches from the beach blanket and of a single stalk of dune grass, the smell of sun-warmed seaweed, the roar of the surf.

At home, the collected shells, pebbles, and driftwood can be the inspiration for any craft project in this chapter. Many of the materials cast up by the sea have a rustic look: driftwood, rounded stones, and clamshells come to mind.

Over the centuries, seashells, seaweed, and pebbles have been the foundation of very elegant designs. In eighteenth-century France the sophisticated rococo style included formal and florid arrangements of shells carved on furniture and woodwork. And for the nobility the height of fashion was a pool and grotto with walls encrusted with mosaics made from the real thing.

Whether you find your treasures on a remote beach or buy them from a shell or crafts supplier, their appeal will be lasting.

Scallop Shell Boxes

Two shells tied together form a precious box—nature's unique packaging for a pair of earrings, a special ring, or other tiny gifts. A stone glued to the interior makes the shell box a perfect paperweight. These shells were found on the beach with the halves still connected by the remnants of the scallop inside. To preserve them they were scraped clean and scrubbed. A coat of acrylic varnish makes them shine and brings out their subtle colors. The rawhide ties, cut from scraps of suede leather, hold the shell halves together. Decorative touches include pieces of dried seaweed, feathers, and other shells.

SIZE

Shells shown are approximately 2" wide

NATURE'S MATERIALS

Pairs of bay scallop or other hinged shells

Feathers, seaweed, driftwood, pebbles, or small shells for decoration

Strips of suede ¼" wide × 12" long

SUPPLIES AND TOOLS

Spray acrylic varnish or varnish and paintbrush

Stiff toothbrush, vegetable brush, or other small, stiff brush

Scissors

White glue or hot-glue gun and glue stick

DIRECTIONS

1. Separate the shell halves and scrub them clean in soapy water with a stiff brush. Let dry.

2. Varnish, either by spraying or brushing on. Let dry.

3. With the shell halves held together, center a suede strip over the hinge and glue it near the hinge on both halves. Glue it again near the open edge of each shell.

4. Tie the suede strip and embellish it with a feather, or glue on a sprig of seaweed or another shell as shown.

Shell-Covered Box

This rococo assemblage of shells is elaborate enough to please Louis XIV himself. The names of shells are just as exotic, from augers and turrets to volutes, strombs, bonnets and frog, trumpet and moon shells. A shell known by one common name on one coast may have another name somewhere else. The hunt for shells becomes even more interesting when you learn about their origin and habitat. For example, a guidebook may reveal that what you thought was a seashell is really the home of a tree snail. The symmetrical design of this shell-covered box is considered formal. For a more rustic approach, arrange the shells in a more casual, random fashion.

SIZE

Box shown is 6" wide × 4" high × 4" deep

NATURE'S MATERIALS

Assorted shells in a variety of sizes and shapes

SUPPLIES AND TOOLS

Unfinished hinged wooden box, 6" × 4" × 4"
Barn-red acrylic paint
Paintbrush
Hot-glue gun and glue stick
White glue

DIRECTIONS

1. Paint the box inside and out with barn-red acrylic paint. Let dry.

2. Position the largest shells on the center of the lid and hot-glue them in place. Turn the box on its side and arrange and glue the shells into position. Repeat for each side of the box.

3. Fill in the empty areas with white glue and press the smaller shells in place. Work on small sections at a time, gluing and placing shells as you go along.

Dresser Set

Before the age of plastic, everyday objects that were "handled," such as tools and kitchen utensils, had wooden handles, carved or turned from handsome hardwoods. Today the search for wooden handles leads to specialty stores or craft galleries, where, thanks to the revival of interest in natural products, wooden brushes, mirrors, and combs can be found. The colors and textures of shells are natural complements to the smooth wood. A cascade of shells tied together with a raffia tassel adds pizzazz to a small clothes brush and a glass bottle. The same shell-and-tassel ornament could decorate a gift package, hang on a Christmas tree, or grace the brim of a summer straw hat.

SIZES

Determined by sizes of accessories

NATURE'S MATERIALS

Assorted shells

Several strands of raffia

Tiny starfish

SUPPLIES AND TOOLS

Wood-backed brushes, mirror, comb

Glass bottle with stopper

Fine sandpaper to remove varnish if necessary

Drill and 1/16" drill bit

Hot-glue gun and glue stick

DIRECTIONS

1. To decorate the backs of the brushes, mirror, and comb, arrange the shells in attractive patterns. If the wood has a varnished or glossy finish, sand just the areas to be glued with fine sandpaper. Hot-glue the shells to the wood.

2. To make the shell cascades and tassels, drill a hole in each shell and tie 1 or 2 strands of raffia to each. Gather the strands and twist them together, arranging the shells into a pleasing cluster. Make a loop of the twisted raffia ends and knot it at the back of the shell cluster. Leave about 2" of raffia loose beyond the knot and trim the ends so they are even. For the finishing touch, hot-glue a tiny starfish to the cluster. Hang the loop over the neck of the bottle and the clothes brush as pictured. Secure the loop and the shells to the clothes brush with a spot of hot glue. Do not glue the shells to the bottle, so the bottle can be washed.

Shell Wreaths

The classic wreath is an impressive way to display a collection of shells. This simple shape is adaptable to many uses, such as the mirror frame and the candleholder shown here. Since these projects involve so many shells of different types it is best to plan ahead, collecting shells on your next beach vacation or making a visit to a craft supply shop or commercial shell supplier to choose from a dazzling selection of shells. The color and pattern of your wreath will vary with the types of shells you use: You may turn out an all-white-and-pink wreath or one softened with the pale orange of "jingle" shells. An ecological note of caution: Some mollusks (the creatures that create and inhabit the shells) are rare and endangered. Collecting only empty shells will assure continued reproduction and replenishment of limited species.

SIZES

As shown:

Large wreath is 14" in diameter

Small wreath is 7" in diameter

NATURE'S MATERIALS

Assorted shells

Sheet moss for small wreath

Spanish moss for large wreath

6"-diameter grapevine wreath for small wreath (to make, see Nature Crafts Basics; or available at craft and floral supply shops)

SUPPLIES AND TOOLS

12"-diameter Styrofoam ring with mirror center (available at craft stores) for large wreath

3"-diameter pillar candle for center of small wreath

Floral wire

Wire cutters

Hot-glue gun and glue stick

DIRECTIONS

1. To make a hanger, cut a length of wire, wrap it around the wreath form, and twist the ends together to form a loop.

2. Using the hot-glue gun, cover the large wreath with Spanish moss and the small wreath with sheet moss.

3. Place the largest shells around each wreath to begin the design. For the smaller wreath, work with the pillar candle standing in the center of the form. Hot-glue the large shells. Fill in around them with medium-sized shells and hot-glue them in place.

4. Finish by hot-gluing the smallest shells in some of the remaining spaces, leaving some of the moss exposed.

Shell Lamp Finials

A touch of nature atop a lamp becomes a miniature sculpture dramatically lit from below. The finial shown in the inset photo is simply a shell glued to a standard brass finial; the other combines two shells glued to a nail hammered into a piece of bark-covered branch. We used a spotted volute with a snail-like moon shell, but a hinged pair of scallop, clam, or oyster shells could also be glued over the nail. The shells pictured are from tropical waters and are brilliantly colored in stripes and dots with softly shaded pale pink linings.

SIZES

Finials shown are 2"–4" tall

NATURE'S MATERIALS

Shell or shells of choice

Small piece of bark-covered branch

Sheet moss

SUPPLIES AND TOOLS

Standard brass finial for single-shell finial

Nut threaded to fit lamp harp for wood-and-shell finial

1½" finishing nail

Drill and a drill bit slightly smaller than diameter of nut and a drill bit slightly smaller than diameter of nail

Wood chisel or utility knife ¼" wide

Hammer

Hot-glue gun and glue stick

DIRECTIONS

Single-Shell Finial

Hot-glue the shell over the top of the finial. While the glue is still hot, stuff some fragments of moss into the base of the shell to cover the glue.

Wood-and-Shell Finial

1. Cut the wood to the desired length (the finial shown used 1¾"). Using the larger bit, drill a hole in the bottom end of the wood slightly smaller in diameter than the nut and the same depth as the nut. Chisel or cut away the sides of the hole so the nut fits tightly. Hammer the nut into the hole. Using the small bit, drill into the top end of the wood about ¼" deep. Hammer the nail into this hole, allowing most of the nail to stick out.

2. Hot-glue the larger shell over the nail. Add moss to the shell opening to cover the glue. Glue the second shell at the base of the first shell.

Seashell Topiaries

Your guests will be delighted with these one-of-a-kind topiary party favors, and you and your family will have a great time scavenging the beach and backyard to gather the components. The designs are free-form, depending on the treasures found— shells, pebbles, sea glass, vines, driftwood—and the imagination of the maker. A touch of a gold felt-tip marker adds polish and shine to the shells, vines, and clay flowerpot base of the topiary shown.

SIZES

Determined by materials used. Topiary featured is 7" tall, including pot

NATURE'S MATERIALS

Assorted seashells, pebbles, sea glass, or other natural materials

Strands of grape or other vine

Spanish moss

SUPPLIES AND TOOLS

2½" clay flowerpots

Styrofoam blocks

Gold paint in jar and paintbrush or felt-tip marker

Sponge or plastic wrap for mottled finish on pot

Sharp knife to cut Styrofoam

Pruning shears

Hot-glue gun and glue stick

DIRECTIONS

1. Cut a piece of Styrofoam to fit tightly into each clay pot. Paint the pot solid gold or paint on patterns, stripes, dots—whatever the spirit suggests. Dab the paint on with a sponge or a wad of plastic wrap, or draw it on with a felt-tip marker.

2. Hot-glue a large shell directly to the foam. Cut a piece of vine with pruning shears. Insert an end of the vine into the Styrofoam, twist it around the shell, and insert the other end into the foam. If vines are not available, substitute small pieces of driftwood or twigs.

3. Glue Spanish moss to cover the Styrofoam and the base of the large shell. Glue smaller shells to the outside of the clay pot. Add more moss to cover the spaces between shells around the pot. Glue on more shells, pebbles, sea glass, or other natural materials if desired. Dress them up with gold paint.

Tablecloth Hold-downs

To ensure that summer breezes won't ruffle the tablecloth on the porch or patio, pin shells to the cloth to weight it down. Pierced-earring backs glued to the shells poke through even the finest damask fabric without damaging it. If your shells are too light-weight, glue a heavy pebble to the inside of each. Shells can be carefully selected to enhance an elegant table setting or can be sturdy surf clamshells used with a homespun cloth on the picnic table. The lower shell shown here is the oversized scallop shell sold in gourmet stores for serving seafood.

SIZES

Determined by shells used

NATURE'S MATERIALS

Assorted seashells

Pebbles (if extra weight is needed)

SUPPLIES AND TOOLS

Cork from bottle

Pierced-earring posts and keepers

Plastic earring washer if necessary to make shell lie flat

Utility knife

Hot-glue gun and glue stick

DIRECTIONS

1. Cut a piece of cork and hot-glue it to the inside of the shell near the top to make a surface level with the outside edge of the shell, using the diagram as a guide.

2. Glue the earring post to the cork. If you are adding a pebble for weight, place it near the bottom of the shell for balance.

3. Poke the post through the tablecloth and secure it with the earring keeper. If the shell does not hang straight, use a plastic earring washer between the cloth and the keeper.

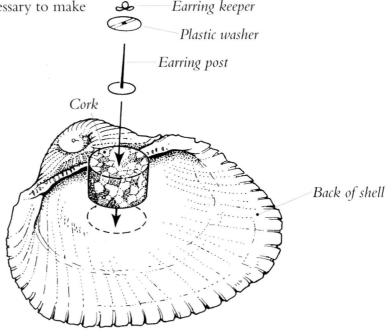

Earring keeper

Plastic washer

Earring post

Cork

Back of shell

Tablecloth Hold-downs

Raffia-and-Shell Tieback

Raffia and seashells complement each other naturally. Here the two work together in a summer-fresh curtain tieback. The size and scale of the tieback depend on the weight and fabric of the window treatment. For heavy canvas curtains make a raffia braid about 1" wide and use large shells. The curtain shown is a cotton-and-polyester sheer, and the tieback braid is only ⅜" wide with scallop shells up to 1½" wide. Make one or a matching pair. Select natural raffia or a color to match your decorating scheme.

SIZE

Determined by curtain. Tieback shown consists of a ⅜"-wide raffia braid 16" long and a raffia tassel 3½" long

NATURE'S MATERIALS

A bundle of raffia

Assorted scallop and clam shells

SUPPLIES AND TOOLS

Clear acrylic spray varnish or varnish and paintbrush

Cup hook, or decorative nail or tack

Hammer

Scissors

Hot-glue gun and glue stick

Scrap of cardboard

Newspaper

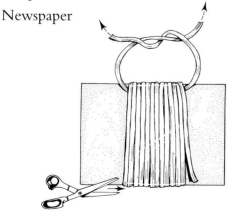

Tassel for Raffia-and-Shell Tieback

DIRECTIONS

1. Spread newspaper on the work surface and spray or brush acrylic varnish onto the shells.

2. Pull strands from the bundle of raffia and divide them into 3 sections for braiding. Make sure the strands are half again as long as the distance around the curtain. Knot at one end and braid. When finished braiding, measure again for the tieback and knot the loose end of the braid. Trim the ends.

3. Decide on the length of the tassel and cut the cardboard to this length by 5" wide. Using the diagram as a guide, wind raffia around the cardboard several times. Slip a single strand of raffia under the loops and tie it in a knot. Cut the raffia along the bottom edge of the cardboard. Cut another length of raffia and wind it around the neck of the tassel and knot in place. Trim the ends of the tassel to make them even. Tie the tassel to the center of the raffia braid.

4. Cut 3 short strands of raffia and hot-glue a shell to each one. Tie the strands to the tassel. Hot-glue a shell to the center of the tassel. Hot-glue a loop of raffia to each end of the tieback.

5. Hammer or screw the cup hook or decorative nail or tack into the side of the window trim. Slip a loop of the tieback onto the hook, wrap the tieback around the curtain, and loop the other end onto the hook.

Raffia-and-Shell
Tieback

Shell Curtain
Holdback

Shell Curtain Holdback

The sculptural shapes, intricate patterns, and wonderful range of colors of seashells look particularly beautiful when used with very simple fabrics in a decorating scheme. Curtains made of canvas, muslin, or linen, and sheers in white or very small patterns take on an air of sophistication in full-length treatments pulled back to the side of the window and held in place with a dramatic seashell. Large spiral shells (for example, those of conchs, volutes, or whelks), similar to the one shown here, or flat shells (for example, those of clams or scallops) work well. Choose the shell size appropriate to the weight of the fabric and the thickness of the curtain when it is pulled to the side of the window. Separate a hinged clam or scallop shell to make a pair.

SIZE

Determined by shell used. Shell shown is
5½" long

NATURE'S MATERIALS

1 shell for each curtain panel

SUPPLIES AND TOOLS

3½"-long piece of wooden dowel ½"–¾"
in diameter

2"-square piece of wood (either ¼" plywood
or lattice)

1" wood screw

4 small-headed ¾" wood screws

Paint to match window trim

Paintbrush

Drill and drill bit slightly smaller than
diameter of wood screws

Screwdriver

Hot-glue gun and glue stick

DIRECTIONS

1. Drill a hole in each corner of the 2"-square backplate. Drill a hole in the center of the backplate and in one end of the dowel. Screw the 1" screw from the back of the backplate, through the center hole, and into the dowel.

2. Paint the backplate and dowel to match the window trim. Let dry.

3. Hot-glue the shell to the free end of the dowel. Let the glue harden.

4. Position the backplate on the window trim and drill into the trim through the corner holes in the backplate. Screw the backplate to the trim. Arrange the curtain in gentle folds over the holdback and around the shell.

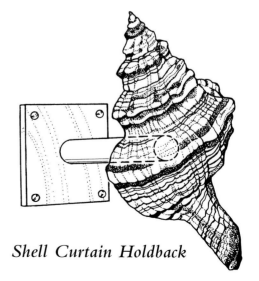

Shell Curtain Holdback

Shell-and-Starfish Curtain Ring Covers

S mall starfish and pearly top shells hide the curtain rings on this cafe curtain. Any number of combinations of different shells in various shapes and colors would be pretty. Because of the weight of the shells, each one must be hooked to a tack in the wood curtain pole and the pole must be firmly affixed to its brackets so it will not twist. The handkerchief linen curtain shown is made with simple inverted pleats for the heading and small plastic rings attached to the pleats. The rings are hung on the tacks in the pole and then covered by the shells. A ready-made curtain can be adapted by sewing rings along the top edge.

SIZES

Pole shown is 24" long; starfish and shells are 2"–4" wide

NATURE'S MATERIALS

Seashells and/or starfish

SUPPLIES AND TOOLS

½"-diameter bone rings (white plastic rings sold as a sewing notion)

½" upholstery tacks

Wooden dowel or curtain pole, length and diameter to fit window and accommodate curtain

Brackets and screws for installing pole

Curtain

Paint for curtain pole

Paintbrush

Hammer

Measuring tape

Needle and thread

DIRECTIONS

1. Install the brackets and cut the curtain pole to the desired length.

2. Paint the pole and the brackets. Let them dry.

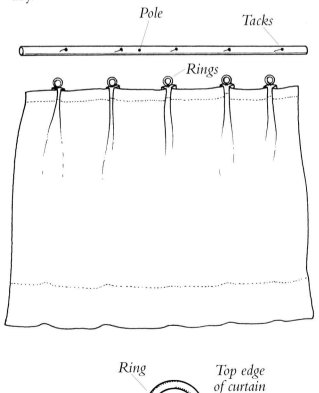

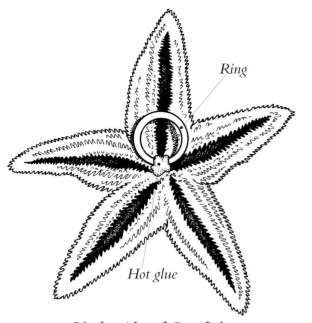

Underside of Starfish

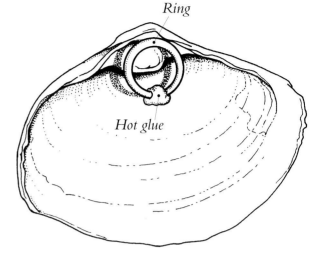

Underside of Shell

3. Measure and mark the positions of the tacks on the pole. Spacing depends on the length of the pole and the number of shells you wish to use. The ones shown are set 5" apart. Referring to the illustration on page 149, hammer tacks into the pole at these points.

4. Sew the plastic rings along the top edge of the curtain, as shown in the illustration, the same distance apart as the tacks.

5. Hot-glue another set of plastic rings to the backs of the shells and starfish as shown in the illustrations above.

6. Hang the curtain by hooking its rings onto the tacks in the wooden curtain pole.

7. Hook the shells and starfish over the tacks to hide them.

Starfish Curtain Pole Finial

Finials add panache to the ends of a curtain pole, in this case a wooden dowel hung on brackets on the surface of the window trim. Dowels come in a range of diameters—the smaller diameters are available in 36" lengths, and the thicker poles, called curtain or closet poles, are much longer. The starfish shown is attached to a rubber tip, the kind designed for the end of a chair leg. The rubber tip is then slipped onto the end of a $\frac{7}{8}$"-diameter curtain pole. For larger-diameter curtain poles the starfish must be glued to a block of wood, which is then screwed to the end of the pole. The size of the finial depends on the size and height of the curtain pole. Clamshells, scallop shells, or smaller shells glued in decorative clusters are alternatives to the starfish but should be large and dramatic enough to balance the overall window and treatment.

SIZE

Determined by choice. Starfish shown is
   6" wide

NATURE'S MATERIALS

2 starfish for each curtain pole

SUPPLIES AND TOOLS

Dowel cut to width of window
   (including trim)

Brackets and screws to install pole

2 rubber chair-leg tips sized to fit dowel

Scrap of wood about 1" square × $\frac{1}{4}$" thick if
   necessary to fill in back of starfish

Hot-glue gun and glue stick

Paint or varnish and paintbrush for dowel
   (optional)

DIRECTIONS

1. Hot-glue the side of a rubber chair-leg tip to the back of the starfish or shell. If the back of the starfish is indented, fill the center with hot glue and adhere a scrap of wood to provide a flat surface for the rubber tip. Hot-glue the side of the rubber tip to the wood. Repeat for the second finial.

2. If desired, paint or varnish the dowel and brackets. Let them dry.

3. Mount the brackets and the curtain pole with the curtain. Slip the finials onto the ends of the rod.

Seasonal Decorations

Seasonal celebrations have always inspired decorations derived from nature, from laurel wreaths to mistletoe. However obscure their origins, these traditional garnishes are an important part of our holidays. The wreath, a classic at Christmas, has become an ideal way to celebrate nature all year round. Evergreens, pinecones, nuts, berries, fruits, vegetables, and flowers all contribute to the festivities. Not only does their natural beauty dress up our homes, but their evocative aromas and symbolic meanings enhance our sense of excitement and joy.

Since it is difficult to preserve in its natural state, the glitter of ice and snow is re-created with gold and silver paint, metallic sparkles, and gilding. The pastel shades of dried flowers bring spring to February and Valentine's Day. The symbols of renewal, the Easter bunny and the decorated egg, mark the arrival of spring. Fall harvest festivals celebrate summer's bounty, and big feasts prepare us for the cold weather to come.

Natural materials can be collected, preserved, and stored for future holidays. The projects that follow can be reused and may themselves become family traditions.

Gilded Magnolia Garland and Sprays

The large, shiny leaves of the southern magnolia, an ornamental tree with huge white flowers seen on lawns throughout the South, are beautiful dried, curling into graceful shapes. Although fragile, they are splendid when sprayed silver and gold, and worth the extra care in handling. Preserved magnolia leaves are a bit more supple and are available from floral suppliers. The garland shown combines dried, gilded magnolia leaves with preserved eucalyptus and pinecones and is festooned with wired copper ribbon. The large leaf spray on page 161 is designed for a wall or door; the smaller one shown here is for a gift package or a tree ornament. The metallic spray paints used on the leaves are also used with natural leaf stencils to transform plain brown paper into princely gift wrap. For instructions and information on drying the leaves, see Nature Crafts Basics.

SIZES

As shown:

Garland is 4' long without eucalyptus sprays at each end

Wall spray is 15" long

Gift spray is 12" wide

NATURE'S MATERIALS

For Garland

12 gold and 8 silver dried and spray-painted magnolia leaves 5"–6" long

3 pinecones approximately 4" long

2–3 bunches of preserved brown eucalyptus

For Wall Spray

6 gold and 3 silver dried and spray-painted magnolia leaves 6"–7" long

4 pinecones approximately 4" long

For Gift Spray

4 dried and gold spray-painted magnolia leaves 5" long; 2 dried and silver spray-painted magnolia leaves 3" long

1 pinecone approximately 3½"

SUPPLIES AND TOOLS

14½ yards of wire-edged sheer copper ribbon 2" wide (approximate lengths: garland, 9 yards; wall spray, 3½ yards; gift spray, 1¾ yards)

Package of heavy-gauge floral wire in 18" lengths

Fine-gauge floral wire

Brown floral tape

Long-nosed pliers for handling heavy-gauge wire

Wire cutters

Pruning shears

Measuring tape

Scissors

Hot-glue gun and glue stick

DIRECTIONS

Garland

1. Overlap the ends of five 18" pieces of heavy floral wire about 5" and twist them together to make 1 length of wire. Wrap the wire with brown floral tape. With pliers, bend a 1¼" loop at each end for hanging. The wire

156

should be about 50" long, including the loops. Adjust this length to suit your space.

2. Form 2 large end sprays: For each, spread out 4 gold and 3 silver leaves in a poinsettia shape and hot-glue them together at the stems. Wrap an 8" piece of fine floral wire around a large pinecone and wire it to the center of the leaves. Cut 20 more 8" pieces of fine floral wire to use when assembling the garland. Using diagram A as a guide, cut three 28" pieces of ribbon and overlap the ends of each to form 3 loops as shown. Pinch the centers of the loops together and wrap them with wire. Cut a 26" and a 36" piece of ribbon and wire them together at the center as shown. Stack the loops on top of these streamers and wire them together. Spread out the loops and the streamers to form a bow. Wire the bow to the back of the leaves. Repeat for the second large spray.

3. Form a small center spray: Cut two 14" pieces of ribbon, stack them, and wire them together at the center. Hot-glue 2 gold leaves together at the stems to form a V. Align a silver leaf in the center and hot-glue it to the

V. Repeat for the other half of the spray. Glue the 2 halves together at the stems as shown in diagram B. Wire a small pinecone to the center of the spray, binding the leaves and ribbons together.

4. Using the 8" pieces of fine floral wire, attach several branches of eucalyptus together to form a 15"-long spray. Repeat for another spray. With the Garland Assembly Diagram on the facing page as a guide, wire the end of each spray to the long garland wire, overlapping the stems on each side of the loop. Repeat with 2 more eucalyptus sprays for the other end of the garland wire. Fill in the space between the large sprays with smaller sprays of eucalyptus, leaving a space at the center for the small gilded leaf spray.

5. Wire the large leaf sprays over the loops at each end of the garland wire. Wire the small leaf spray to the center of the main wire. Trim the ends of the ribbon streamers into inverted Vs. Fill in with eucalyptus leaves as needed. This garland can be hung on a stair rail, as shown, or as a swag above a doorway, or on the face of a mantel, under the shelf.

Magnolia Garland

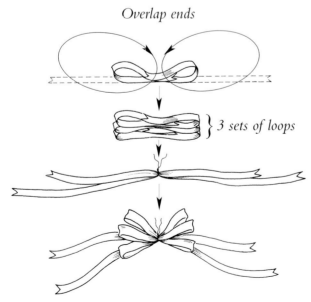

Overlap ends

3 sets of loops

A. Ribbon Loops and Streamers

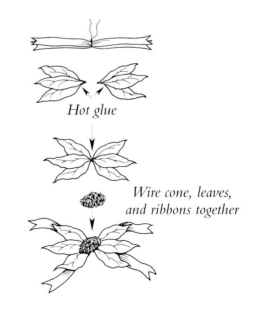

Hot glue

Wire cone, leaves, and ribbons together

B. Center Spray of Garland

158

Wall Spray

1. Cut nine 18" pieces of heavy floral wire and wrap them with brown floral tape. Hot-glue a taped wire to the back of each leaf, along the center stem of the leaf. Arrange the leaves in a long cluster, beginning with the bottom leaves, and wind the wires together. With fine floral wire, wire the pinecones into a pleasing arrangement at the top of the spray of leaves. Trim the ends of the heavy wires and wrap them with floral tape. Bend the wrapped ends into a loop for hanging.

2. Cut an 18" length of fine floral wire. Using the Ribbon Loops and Streamers diagram on the facing page as a guide, cut three 22" pieces of ribbon and overlap the ends of each to form 3 loops. Pinch the centers together and wrap them with wire. Cut the remaining ribbon into 3 even pieces. Stack the loops on top of these streamers and wire them all together at the center. Spread the loops and the streamers into a bow and wire it to the back of the spray. Trim the ends of the ribbon into an inverted V.

Gift Spray

1. Hot-glue 2 gold leaves together at the stems to form a V. Align a silver leaf in the center and hot-glue it to the V. Repeat for the other half of the spray. Glue the 2 halves together at the stems. (See the Center Spray of Garland illustration as a guide.)

2. Cut a 16" piece of fine floral wire. Cut one 14", two 12", and two 10" pieces of ribbon. Stack the ribbons with the longest on the bottom and the shortest on top and center them. Pinch the ribbons together at the center and wrap with wire, forming a bow. Wire the center of the bow to the center back of the leaves. Spread out the ribbons in a fan shape. Hot-glue them in spots to the backs of the leaves to keep them in place. Add ribbon loops to enhance a larger package. Trim the ends of the ribbons into inverted Vs.

3. Wire the pinecone to the center of the leaves and twist the wire at the back. Use the wire ends to attach the spray to the gift.

Garland Assembly Diagram

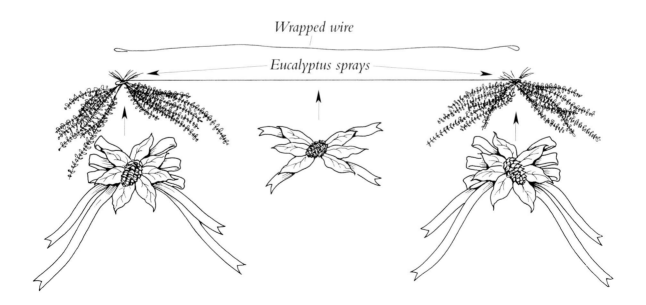

Wrapped wire

Eucalyptus sprays

Gilded Gift Wrap

Give a gift in a not-so-plain brown wrapping. Ordinary shipping paper gleams with pattern and texture laid down with silver, gold, and brown spray paint. Scattered leaves and pine needles act as natural stencils, leaving their lacy outlines by blocking the paint. This is the same technique that was used for the Stenciled Leaf Tray on page 54. See page 159 for instructions to make the Wall Spray shown on the facing page.

SIZE

Determined by amount of paper needed

NATURE'S MATERIALS

Assorted leaves, twigs, and evergreen sprays

SUPPLIES AND TOOLS

Brown shipping paper
Spray paint: gold, silver, and dark brown
Several 1" pebbles
Newspaper

DIRECTIONS

1. Spread out newspaper in a well-ventilated work space. Place a large sheet of brown paper on the newspaper. Lay large leaves and evergreen sprays face down (so they lie flatter) on the paper.

2. Spray around the edges of the leaves and the stems with dark brown paint. Work with a light touch, spraying soft clouds of paint without saturating or completely covering the paper. If the leaves shift while spraying, weight their centers with pebbles. Let dry.

3. Arrange the smaller leaves and branches and spray with gold and silver paints as desired. Let dry.

Handmade Valentines

Bring spring to deep midwinter with valentines of handmade paper textured with pressed flowers and dried herbs. Chubby hearts with cupids and rosebuds take their shapes from candy and jelly molds. Pressed pansies, delphinium blossoms, ferns, and scented herbal leaves waft charm and romance. A scattering of composition gold leaf is part of the paper and bestows the final gilded touch on these gifts of love. For instructions and information on making paper and pressing flowers, see Nature Crafts Basics.

SIZES

As shown:

Large molded hearts are 3½" × 3½"

Small molded hearts are 1½" × 1½"

Large cards are 6" × 4½"

Small cards are 3½" × 3¾"

NATURE'S MATERIALS

Dried and pressed flowers, herbs for dyes and texture in paper and for final decorations

SUPPLIES AND TOOLS

Dyed paper pulp (see Nature Crafts Basics)

Clear plastic candy molds in desired shapes and sizes

Small strainer

Small piece of sponge

Acrylic paint in colors of choice

Composition gold leaf

Gold-leaf adhesive size

Small paintbrush

Assorted small pieces of ribbon

Hair blow-dryer

Dinner knife

White tacky glue

Hot-glue gun and glue stick (optional)

DIRECTIONS

Molded Hearts

1. Make and dye paper pulp according to the instructions in Nature Crafts Basics. Strain the pulp and spoon it generously into the candy molds. Use a damp sponge to press the pulp against the walls of the mold, removing the excess water. Add more pulp to fill in areas as needed. Let dry 12 hours until hardened. To speed drying, you can hold a blow-dryer over the pulp. Remove the pulp from the mold. Dry the face of the molded pulp with the dryer to remove any dampness.

2. Paint details on the cupids or flowers. Following the manufacturer's directions, brush size on the molded heart and gild it with small pieces of composition gold leaf. Decorate with pressed flowers, leaves, or dried flowers, glued on with white tacky glue. Make ribbon loop hangers and glue them on.

Valentine Cards

1. Following the instructions in Nature Crafts Basics, make sheets of paper in 2 different colors. For each card, fold a piece of paper in half.

2. Using a heart-shaped mold as a guide, trace a heart onto the back of another sheet of paper with a dinner knife. Carefully tear out the heart along the scored line. Glue heart, pressed flowers and leaves, and bits of composition gold leaf to the card.

Patinated Wreath

Nature's process of corrosion is given a boost with copper paint and an accompanying treatment to hasten the green, antiqued effect called verdigris, or patina. While the copper turns green, the chemicals used in the treatment form crystals that make the surface sparkle. The wreath pictured is made from grapevines, and the fragile dried maple leaves are backed with a network of hot glue to give them strength before they are treated. For instructions and information on drying plant materials and making the wreath see Nature Crafts Basics, or you can buy a ready-made vine wreath from a craft supply shop. Look for a patina kit, which contains the paint and chemicals, in art supply stores.

SIZE

Wreath shown is 10" in diameter

NATURE'S MATERIALS

10"-diameter grapevine wreath

8 or 9 small dried maple leaves or other leaves

SUPPLIES AND TOOLS

Modern Options™ Copper Topper (paint)

Modern Options Patina Green (chemicals)

Foam paintbrush

Disposable bristle paintbrush

Rubber gloves

(The above items are all contained in the Modern Options Kit; Copper Topper and Patina Green are also available in 4-ounce bottles)

Hot-glue gun and glue stick

Newspaper

Gold spray paint (optional)

DIRECTIONS

1. Spread out newspaper in a well-ventilated work space. Put on rubber gloves. Using the foam brush, paint the wreath with copper paint. With the disposable brush, apply Patina Green, following the manufacturer's directions. Repeat the treatment for additional coverage.

2. With the hot-glue gun, outline the backs of the leaves with thin lines of glue. Crisscross the leaf to form a strengthening network. Allow the glue to harden.

3. Paint the leaves with copper paint using the foam brush or spray them with gold paint for a slightly lighter color. Apply a coat of Patina Green. Let dry. It will take several hours for the leaves to turn green. Repeat Patina Green if desired and let dry. Hot-glue the leaves to the wreath.

Patinated Eggs

Dress the holiday tree with hollow eggshells that have been patinated. The designs are cut out of masking tape and applied before the chemical treatment. When the masking tape is removed the copper gleams through. A coat of Mod-Podge strengthens the eggs so that they will last many seasons. You may wish to display the eggs all year long. Chicken eggs work fine, but for greater impact try duck or goose eggs, if available.

SIZE

Determined by the eggs used

NATURE'S MATERIALS

Eggs, uncooked

SUPPLIES AND TOOLS

Modern Options Copper Topper (paint)

Modern Options Patina Green (chemicals)

Foam paintbrush

Disposable bristle paintbrush

Rubber gloves

(The items above are all contained in the
   Modern Options Kit; Copper Topper
   and Patina Green are also available in
   4-ounce bottles)

White flat primer paint, spray or brush-on

Mod-Podge matte finish

Perle cotton, embroidery floss, or string for
   hanger

⅜"-diameter sequin for each hanger

Corrugated cardboard

Long straight pins

Skewer or knitting needle

White tissue paper

Masking tape or shaped peel-off stickers

Newspaper

Fine paintbrush for touch-up (optional)

DIRECTIONS

1. Make a stand for holding each egg while you're working on it by pushing 4 straight pins through from the back of the cardboard. Slant the pins outward so they cradle the egg.

2. Empty each egg following the instructions for Blown Eggs, below. To reinforce the eggshell brush a coat of Mod-Podge over the whole egg and adhere small pieces of tissue paper while the Mod-Podge is still wet. Cover

❧ Blown Eggs ❧

For projects involving nonedible dyes, emptied eggs are recommended. Blowing out the whites and yolks of uncooked eggs is the best way to keep the shells intact. The eggs will then last indefinitely if stored in a cardboard egg carton. Using a pushpin or a sharp nail, poke a hole in each end of the egg. Insert a skewer or a knitting needle into the hole at one end of the egg and swirl it around to break the yoke. Blow the contents of the egg into a bowl and discard it or save it for an omelette. With your finger covering one hole, fill the egg with cold water and shake it. Pour out the water and rinse again. Set the egg on the skewer or knitting needle resting in a tall glass and let it dry, or place the egg on a warm (not hot) radiator overnight until it dries.

the hole in the bottom of the egg. Let dry.

3. Spread newspaper over the work surface in a well-ventilated area. Paint the egg with white primer. Let dry.

4. Put on the rubber gloves. Using the foam brush, cover the egg with copper paint. Let dry about 10 minutes. Apply masking tape cutouts or shaped stickers to the egg. With the disposable brush, apply Patina Green, following the manufacturer's directions. Let dry.

5. Remove the tape or stickers to reveal the copper surface. Touch up any smudges with copper paint and a fine brush. (Another technique for creating polka dots is to paint them on with a cotton-tipped swab and copper paint after the Patina Green has dried.)

6. For the hanger, make a loop from a 7" length of perle cotton, embroidery floss, or string and knot the ends. Cut through the sequin, from the rim to the center, and slip the sequin over the loop just above the knot. Apply hot glue to the sequin and the knot and press them to the top of the egg, pushing the knot into the blow hole.

Twig Easter Basket

A basket to welcome spring or the Easter bunny is made from twigs, moss, and delicate dried flowers. With its raftlike platform base and open, fencelike sides, it makes a festive holiday centerpiece filled with eggs colored with vegetable dyes. Use it later as a planter or to display a treasured porcelain egg or bird. In summer, pile it with fresh fruits. The dimensions given are only a suggestion. Make your basket any size, as rustic and irregular as you wish.

SIZE

Basket shown is 6" wide × 6" deep × 11" high

NATURE'S MATERIALS

About 18 twigs with bark, approximately 6" long × ¼" in diameter

About 22 twigs with bark, approximately 6" long × ½" in diameter

3 lengths of 24" grapevine for the handle

Sheet moss

Dried pink larkspur or stock

Dried yellow rosebuds

Strawflowers

SUPPLIES AND TOOLS

6" square of cardboard

Fine floral wire

Wire cutters

Pruning shears

Hot-glue gun and glue stick

DIRECTIONS

1. Soak the 3 lengths of grapevine in warm water for about an hour. These will be used for the handle of the basket.

2. While the grapevines are soaking, make the base of the basket. Lay the cardboard square on your work surface. Using it as a guide, place two ½"-diameter twigs on opposite sides of the square. With the glue gun, glue two ¼"-diameter twigs perpendicular to the ends of the two ½"-diameter twigs to form a square. Set aside the cardboard square. Continue to glue ¼"-diameter twigs parallel to these to form a platform. Lay the twigs next to one another.

3. To form the sides of the basket, glue a ½"-diameter twig across each end of the platform. Add the rest of the ½"-diameter twigs, alternating from one side to the other, as if you were building a log cabin, until all the sides are 4 or 5 twigs high.

4. Remove the grapevines from the water. Twist and bend them into a handle shape. Weave curly tendrils in and around the handle and secure all strands together at each end with floral wire. Position the handle at least 2" inside the basket, centered on opposite sides. Secure the handle with wire.

5. Line the inside and the rim of the basket with strips of sheet moss, attaching them with spots of hot glue. From the outside of the basket, cover the wired ends of the handle with moss. Glue 6" lengths of larkspur or stock along the moss-covered rim of the basket. Glue 2 strawflowers and a dried rosebud to the rim of the basket at each end of the handle.

6. Fill the basket with more moss to make a nest for Easter eggs.

Easter Egg Bunny

The egg, one of nature's truly ingenious creations, has come to symbolize rebirth, fertility, the source of life, and the promise of spring in religions throughout the world. How fitting that the rabbit, the deliverer of Easter eggs and a prolific symbol of fertility in its own right, is now made from an egg—a nice, fat brown egg with floppy ears and hopping big feet. If you're lucky you may find domestic chickens and ducks that lay natural green eggs, or use white eggs and give the bunny dried sage or bay leaf ears. This one has the bark from the paper birch for both ears and feet, and a dried globe amaranth flower for a tail.

SIZE

Determined by the egg used

NATURE'S MATERIALS

Brown egg, uncooked

Birch bark (from a fallen branch or firewood)
  Note: Instead of bark, you may use light cardboard for feet and ears

1 dried globe amaranth

SUPPLIES AND TOOLS

Fine felt-tip markers: pink and blue

Tracing paper

Scissors

White tacky glue

Hot-glue gun and glue stick

Pencil

DIRECTIONS

1. Empty each egg following the instructions for Blown Eggs on page 166.

2. Trace the patterns provided for the feet and the ears onto tracing paper and cut them out. Place the patterns on bark or cardboard and trace them with a pencil. Trace 2 sets of ears. Cut out all the pieces. Glue the 2 sets of ears together with white tacky glue to make them stiffer. The pinkish inside of the bark serves as the inside of the ear; the white bark is on the back. Hot-glue the feet and the ears to the egg.

3. With pencil lightly draw the eyes, nose, and mouth on the egg. You may erase and redraw if necessary. When you're satisfied with the bunny's facial features, color the eyes, nose, and mouth with blue and pink markers.

4. Glue on the globe amaranth tail.

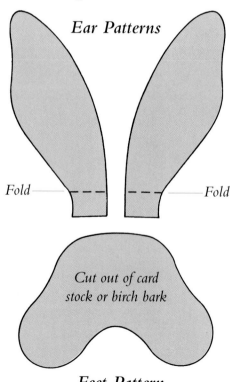

Ear Patterns

Fold — — — *Fold*

Cut out of card stock or birch bark

Feet Pattern

Leaf-Resist, Dyed, and Gilded Eggs

Onion skins, carrot tops, Italian parsley, and a pinch of mint leaves are the natural ingredients for resist-printed eggs. Various shades of yellow to brown are achieved with dye brewed from the papery outer skins of onions. For the resist patterns, leaves are pressed against the eggs during the coloring process and prevent the color from reaching the eggs. Another bonus is that the dye can be brewed and the eggs cooked at the same time. If it's winter, without a grass patch or herb garden in sight, search the grocery store for the produce you'll need. The pink egg is colored with a dye called cochineal, made from an insect found on cacti. Although originally thought to be a berry and used medicinally, cochineal is not edible and is most frequently used for dying wool. It is available at yarn stores. Use cochineal on emptied or blown eggs only. The gilded egg in front of the basket glows with flakes of composition gold leaf. For instructions and information on making dyes from natural materials see Nature Crafts Basics.

SIZE

Determined by the eggs used

NATURE'S MATERIALS

White extra-large or jumbo eggs, uncooked

Shapely leaves from carrot tops, Italian parsley, mint, or other herbs

Dry, papery skins of 6 onions (*Hint:* When buying onions, scoop extra onion paper from the bottom of the bin into the bag)

2 tablespoons of cochineal

White of 1 uncooked egg (for gilding)

SUPPLIES AND TOOLS

6" squares of cheesecloth, gauze, or nylon stocking

Composition gold leaf

Small paintbrush

Plastic-coated twist ties

Large slotted spoon

Heatproof glass or stainless-steel pot

Heatproof glass or stainless-steel bowl

Tablespoon

White vinegar

Cake rack

Rubber gloves

Soft paper towel or cloth

DIRECTIONS

Leaf-Resist Egg

1. Lay a sprig of leaves on the egg. Lay a square of gauze over the egg and twist it tight at the back with a twist tie.

2. Make a packet of gauze containing the papery onion skins and close it with a twist tie.

3. Place the egg and the onion skin packet in a pot of cold water and bring to a boil. Simmer 30–60 minutes. Let the egg cool in the water 5–10 minutes. Using the slotted spoon, take the egg out of the dye bath and

remove the gauze and the leaf sprig. Reserve the dye in the pot if you want the leaf print to be colored. Gently wipe excess moisture off the egg with a soft paper towel or cloth. Let the egg dry on the cake rack.

4. To color the leaf print light yellow, place the egg back in the onion dye bath for a few minutes only. Leave it in longer for a darker brown color.

Pink Egg

1. Empty the egg following the instructions for Blown Eggs on page 166.

2. Place 2 heaping tablespoons of cochineal into a gauze square and close it with a twist tie. Place the packet of dye in a bowl and pour 2 cups of boiling water onto the packet. Wearing rubber gloves, remove the packet with the slotted spoon when the dye is a deep cranberry color. Squeeze out the excess water and save the packet for reuse, as the cochineal is very strong. Add 1 tablespoon of white vinegar to the dye bath.

3. With the slotted spoon, lower the egg into the dye for a minute or so, turning it frequently for even color. Since the egg has been emptied, it will float unless you hold it under with a spoon until it fills up with dye. Remove the egg with a slotted spoon and hold it so the dye runs out. Let the egg dry on the cake rack.

Gilded Egg

1. Empty the egg following the instructions for Blown Eggs on page 166. Set aside the egg white from another egg.

2. Color the egg in a dye bath or leave it natural. Let it dry on the cake rack.

3. With dry fingers, place a sheet of composition gold leaf on a plate and break it into interesting shapes about ¾" wide.

4. Brush a small amount of egg white onto the shell. Arrange the gold leaf on the egg, smoothing it in place with your finger and leaving cracks to allow the surface of the egg to show through. Let dry.

Cornucopia Centerpiece

A ready-made horn-shaped basket forms the base for a centerpiece that will look festive on a holiday table or mantel, or hung from a hook on the wall by the loop at its open end. Fill it with leaves, dried pods and berries, and small gourds for Thanksgiving or with lady apples, kumquats, and greens for Christmas. The decorations may change with the seasons, from the wintry pepper berries, rose hips, and lotus pods shown here to dried flowers and grasses for a summery look. For instructions and information on drying plant materials see Nature Crafts Basics.

SIZE

Cornucopia shown is 8" wide × 16" long

NATURE'S MATERIALS

Grapevine cornucopia basket, from craft
   supply shop
60 tiny hemlock cones
15 dried galax leaves
10 small white lotus pods
6 sprigs of small rose hips
4 sprigs of pepper berries
Sheet moss

SUPPLIES AND TOOLS

Scissors
Hot-glue gun and glue stick

DIRECTIONS

1. With the glue gun, attach the sheet moss randomly around the open end of the cornucopia, leaving sections of the rim exposed.

2. Glue lotus pods in a cluster on each side of cornucopia, slightly below the rim. Arrange the galax leaves around the lotus pods and glue them in place.

3. Fill in the exposed areas of the rim with clusters of hemlock cones.

4. Glue a cluster of pepper berries on each side and a few sprigs of rose hips around the rim.

Pinecone Flower Vase

A plain glass jar disguised by pinecones becomes a rustic-looking water vase for fresh-cut flowers. The almonds and filberts on the rim of the vase came from a grocery store, but acorns, hickory nuts, and other wild materials found locally could be used. The handles of the vase are cut from the rim of a plastic lid from a deli take-out container and then wrapped with moss. The worlds of plastic and nature happily coexist here and no one will notice.

SIZE

Pinecone vase shown is 7½" high × 8" in diameter

NATURE'S MATERIALS

10 pine or other tree cones 6" long × 2" in diameter (we used Norway spruce cones)

30 almonds in their shells

10 filberts in their shells

Sheet moss

SUPPLIES AND TOOLS

1 quart-size glass jar

1 plastic lid from a quart-size plastic take-out container

Fine floral wire

Large rubber band

Wire cutters

Scissors

Hot-glue gun and glue stick

DIRECTIONS

1. To attach the pinecones to the jar, stand the jar on your work surface. Try fitting the cones around the jar first and select the sizes that will provide the most coverage. Any gaps that show the glass jar will be covered with sheet moss. Using the glue gun, glue the pinecones upright onto the jar so their bases just touch the table surface. The cones can be pushed together gently so the cone scales overlap slightly. Press each cone in place until it is secure. Slip a large rubber band around the cones to hold them in place until the glue sets.

2. Glue a row of almonds flat against the jar just above the pinecones, with the pointed ends up. Glue a second row of almonds directly on top of the first row of almonds, with the almonds placed on their edges, again with the pointed ends up.

3. Glue sheet moss around and inside the lip of the jar to cover any exposed glass. If glass shows at the base of the jar, glue sheet moss around the bottom of the jar as well.

4. Glue filberts in a ring around the lip of the jar.

5. With scissors, cut the plastic lid in half and cut out the centers, so that just the rim of each half remains. These will be the handles of the vase. Wrap each half with floral wire. Using the glue gun, cover the wrapped rims with sheet moss. Glue one end of the handle to the jar by inserting it between 2 pinecones. Bend the upper end down and glue it just below the row of filberts. Repeat with the other handle.

Spiral Topiary

A textured palette of subtle greens, yellows, and faded cranberry celebrates the seasons in an unusual way. Much of the color in this topiary comes from the many kinds of moss and lichen used, all of which are available commercially. Included are Spanish moss (beige or green), reindeer moss (green or white), and the striking chartreuse moss. Black lichen, white on the reverse side, climbs the center stem. Lichen is also available in red, pink, and purple. Sprigs of dried hydrangea provide the spots of pale blue-green and soft red. Each season brings a different array of natural materials. Sponge mushrooms and lots of shells collected on the beach are the ornaments here, topped off with a large dried starfish.

SIZE

Spiral topiary shown is 3' tall

NATURE'S MATERIALS

3'-long branch with bark and lichen, about 2" in diameter

Grapevine spiral, from craft supply shop

Mosses: reindeer, giant reindeer, Spanish, lace, chartreuse

Lichen: black, red, pink, or purple

Sprigs of dried hydrangea

Sponge mushrooms

Seashells   Starfish   Twigs

SUPPLIES AND TOOLS

1 large clay flowerpot, approximately 12" in diameter

1 plastic pot to fit into clay flowerpot

Blocks of Styrofoam

Plaster of Paris

Floral wire

2 yards of 3"-wide wire-edged ribbon

Knife for cutting Styrofoam

Wire cutters   Scissors

Hot-glue gun and glue stick

DIRECTIONS

1. Place the branch upright in the plastic pot. Brace it with chunks of Styrofoam wedged in the bottom of the pot. Mix the plaster of Paris according to the directions on the package and pour it around the branch, filling the plastic pot ¾ full. Let it harden overnight.

2. With floral wire, attach the inner end of the grapevine spiral to the top of the branch. Hot-glue it to hold it securely in place. When the glue is hard, expand the spiral in coils around the branch and anchor the bottom end to the edge of the plastic pot with wire and hot glue.

3. Hot-glue seashells along the spiral. Add mosses and fungi. Fill in any spaces with Spanish moss and chartreuse moss. Decorate the spiral with twigs and sprigs of hydrangea. Continue adding the decorative material to the spiral until it looks even and well balanced.

4. Place the plastic pot inside the clay pot and fill with Spanish moss to cover the plaster of Paris and to flow over the edges of the clay pot. Finish the top of the spiral by hot-gluing on a dried starfish, a beautiful shell, or other natural decoration. Tie a large wired-ribbon bow and and hot-glue it onto the clay pot.

Golden Grapevine Wreath

This golden wreath is a wispy tangle of dried leaves, raffia, and silver-lace vine woven among the strands of grapevine. A final spray of gold paint adds sparkle and luster. If you have shells, dried fruits, or dried flowers, they can be tucked in among the strands of gold for a more elaborate version of this wreath. Make your own wreath or purchase one from a florist or craft supply store. For instructions and information on making a grapevine wreath see Nature Crafts Basics.

SIZE

Grapevine wreath shown is 28" in diameter

NATURE'S MATERIALS

Grapevine wreath with leaves left on
Silver-lace vine
Raffia

SUPPLIES AND TOOLS

Gold spray paint
Pruning shears
Newspaper

DIRECTIONS

1. Twist silver-lace vine between the vines of the grapevine wreath.

2. If you are using fresh vines, hang the wreath in a dry place out of direct light for 2–3 weeks to allow it to dry.

3. When the wreath has dried, add strands of raffia, weaving them among the vines and letting some ends fly loose.

4. Spread out newspaper in a well-ventilated work space. Place the wreath on the newspaper and spray it with gold paint. Let dry thoroughly.

Pumpkin Centerpiece

Light up your harvest table with several carved squash and gourds in addition to the traditional pumpkin. The cutout patterns include cookie cutter hearts and diamonds, apple corer circles, and free-form slits following the natural pattern of the gourd. To give them a polished look, these candlelit lanterns have been cut for scooping out at the base instead of at the top, but if you intend to leave the candles burning throughout the evening, you may want to make the tops removable, in case the candles begin to smoke. Filling out the centerpiece are smaller pumpkins and round gourds, which serve as flower holders—or as bowls for a first course of pumpkin soup. A trail of ivy vines ties it all together.

SIZES

Assorted

NATURE'S MATERIALS

Assorted pumpkins, squash (winter, acorn, spaghetti), and gourds

Fresh flowers

Ivy

SUPPLIES AND TOOLS

Cookie cutters in heart and diamond shapes

Apple corer

Melon baller or sharp-edged spoon

Sharp kitchen knife

Large metal spoon with strong handle

Utility knife (an X-acto knife with #11 blade works well)

Red or orange felt-tip marker

Assorted candle stubs 3"–6" long

DIRECTIONS

1. To make the lanterns, cut out the bottom (or top, if desired) of each pumpkin, squash, or gourd by circling deep around the base (or stem) with a sharp kitchen knife. Lift out the cut section and remove the seeds and pulp from it. With the large spoon, scoop out the inside. With the large end of the melon baller or a sharp-edged spoon, scrape the inside walls clean. Save the seeds and dry them for eating or for a seed embroidery project, such as the one on page 41.

2. Plan your design for each pumpkin, squash, and gourd. Using the cookie cutters as templates, draw it onto the surface with the felt-tip marker. You can try to push the cookie cutter into the sides to make an outline to cut by, but the cutters often are not strong enough to penetrate the skin. Cut out the designs with the kitchen knife and use the utility knife to clean up the edges of any uneven cuts.

3. Use the apple corer to cut about ⅜" into the base of the pumpkin, squash, or gourd to make a cylindrical hole for the candle. If you have made the access from the bottom, this is easy to do because you cut into the center of the removed piece. Use the utility knife or a spoon to clean out the candle hole as necessary. A toothpick inserted in the bottom of the candle will make it more secure in the hole. Lower the pumpkin, squash, or gourd over the candle.

4. To make the flower holders, cut out the lids and clean the insides of the pumpkins, squash, or gourds as described in step 1. Fill them ¾ full with water and insert small bunches of flowers. Softer-walled squash may become soggy sooner than others, so fill them just before your guests are due to arrive. Intersperse them among the lanterns and weave vines of ivy in and out of the arrangement. If you are leaving the centerpiece on display for several days, place all the items on a tray to protect the tabletop.

Mantel Garland

Nature's bounty is celebrated and displayed at the fireplace or dining table, the focal points of our holiday traditions. The fall harvest is symbolized here by long-lasting gourds, ornamental corn, and shafts of wheat in a garland that can be used as a centerpiece at Thanksgiving. Gourds and several varieties of corn—such as Wampum, Chinook, and strawberry popcorn (used here)—show up at roadside vegetable stands in September. (See the discussion of ornamental corn on page 183.) Many grains are available from the garden or from suppliers of dried plants. Golden wheat, black-bearded wheat, and oats all add texture and grace to dried displays. For instructions and information on drying plant materials see Nature Crafts Basics.

SIZE

Garland shown is 36" long

NATURE'S MATERIALS

Golden wheat with stems about 18" long

12 small ears of dried corn in a variety of colors, with some husks left on

6 galax leaves

4 branches of rose hips

3 gourds about 3" in diameter

3 stems of cockscomb

3 stems of yarrow

2 pinecones

Raffia

SUPPLIES AND TOOLS

Styrofoam block, carved into a mound about 3" high × 6" in diameter

Fourteen 3" floral picks

Two 6" floral picks

Fine floral wire

Wire cutters

Scissors

DIRECTIONS

1. Place the Styrofoam mound on the work surface. This is the center of the arrangement.

2. Cut 2 bunches of wheat to the desired length if necessary (depending on the size of the mantel or table) and wire each bunch onto a 6" floral pick. Insert a bunch on opposite sides of the foam mound.

3. Lay 3 or 4 ears of corn along each bunch of wheat and tie them to the wheat with raffia. Trim the ends of the raffia.

4. Using the photos as guides, fill in the center of the arrangement with gourds, cockscomb, yarrow, pinecones, and the remaining corn. To make the gourds easier to attach, insert a 3" pick into the base of each gourd. Wire a pick to each ear of corn and to the pinecones.

5. Cut additional bunches of wheat with shorter stems, corn husks, and galax leaves to fill in any spaces and to cover any picks that might show. For the final touch of color add some sprigs of rose hips.

❋ Ornamental Corn ❋

Many varieties of corn long noted for their decorative kernels are now available as ornamental grasses for the garden. The stalks, leaves, and silky tassels grow quickly, are showy, and provide texture, color, and screening. In the fall the plants can be cut down and bundled for harvest displays. The new names, Chinook and Wampum, are a reflection of their Indian corn ancestors. Chinook seed produces plants about 6' tall with dark maroon, tan, and yellow ears. Wampum has smaller ears with great color variety and multihued tassels for use in dried arrangements. Strawberry popcorn's ears are short and fat, and are covered with deep red–purple kernels, which can be popped for a healthy snack.

Braided-Wheat Ornaments

Wheat weavings are a common tradition in many cultures, as ancient symbols of fertility and the harvest and as tokens of courtship. The designer of these wheat weavings was inspired by the memory of the ornaments and decorations her Scandinavian grandmother used to make. Although other grains, such as oats or rye, may be used, wheat is most readily available, either from a local farm or by mail. Ornamental grasses, so popular in many residential gardens, may also be used for these projects. Traditionally, the angel and the heart-shaped Mordiford (a design from the village of Mordiford, England) were tied with red or white string. Since it is easier to control, fine floral wire is used here and then covered with strands of red-dyed raffia. The Mordiford is made with braided straw ribbon called Scandi, available in rolls from craft supply stores.

SIZES

Shown clockwise from left:

Angel is 5" wide × 5" high

Heart Mordiford is 3½" wide × 9" high

Wheat bundle is 9" high

Star is 2½" across

NATURE'S MATERIALS

For Angel

Ten 8" wheat straws with heads

Fourteen 5" wheat straws without heads
  (6 for arms, 8 for wings)

Strand of red raffia

For Heart Mordiford

Twenty-one 10" wheat straws with heads

10-mm Scandi braid: two 12" pieces and two
  2" pieces

Strand of red raffia

For Wheat Bundle

Twelve 9" wheat straws with heads

For Star

11¼" piece of wheat straw without head

Strand of red raffia

SUPPLIES AND TOOLS

Red ½"-diameter wood or plastic bead
  for angel

Fine craft wire

Wire cutters

Scissors

Hot-glue gun and glue stick

Long, shallow pan of warm water

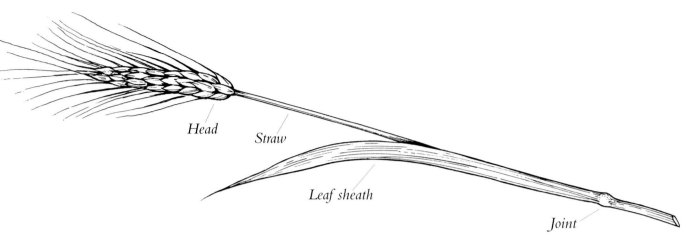

Head　*Straw*

Leaf sheath

Joint

Wheat Stalk

DIRECTIONS

General

To clean the wheat, cut the straw above the first joint and remove the leaf sheath. Sort according to the size of the head and the diameter of the straw. Select the wheat needed for a project and soak it in warm water for 15–30 minutes in a long, shallow pan. Soak only the amount of straw required. Oversoaking causes the straw to become discolored, limp, and sticky. Straw cannot be soaked twice, because it will become brittle. Wheat heads left damp for 2–3 days will sprout, a testament to their reserved energy but not pleasing in the final design. In fact, the earliest versions of these ornaments were kept indoors over the winter and cast into the fields in spring to ensure a successful growing season.

Angel

1. Soak the straw, following the general directions above.

2. For the skirt, arrange 10 straws with heads in a fan shape and wrap them with wire ¼" above the heads, forming the waist.

3. For the wings, wrap wire around the center of a bundle of 8 headless straws, leaving 1½" of loose wire at the ends.

4. To form the body of the angel, slip the cut ends of as many of the straws from the skirt as will fit up through the red bead, fold the ends down the back, and wrap with wire at the waist (see photo). If the hole is too small for all the straws, bend the extras over at either side of the bead. After the waist is wired, go back and glue the bent extras to the side of the bead as hair.

5. Slip the wings through the straws that form the torso and wire in place just under the red bead.

6. To make the arms, divide the remaining 6 headless straws into 3 sections and braid them. Wrap each end with a small piece of wire. Hot-glue the center of the arms just under the red bead to cover the wire holding the wings. Hot-glue the other ends (the hands) to the front of the skirt.

7. Wrap a piece of red raffia around the waist to cover the wire.

Heart Mordiford

1. Cut two 12" lengths of wire. Lay one 12" length of Scandi braid on the work surface. Hot-glue the 2 strands of wire down the center of the braid, forming a wire "spine." Layer the second length of Scandi braid over the first to cover the wire. Let the glue set. Bend the doubled braid into a heart shape with the cut ends at the bottom. Wrap wire around the bottom point of the heart.

2. Soak the straw, following the general directions on the facing page. Divide the straws into 2 groups, one of 5 and one of 16 straws. Lay 5 straws on the work surface. Place the heart over the 5 straws with the straw heads 1" below the bottom point of the heart. Lay the 16 straws on top of the heart in the same position. Wrap wire around the straws ½" above the heart and at the base of the heart. Wrap wire around the straw just below the top of the heart to hold the heart in place.

3. Working at the top of the heart, divide the ends of the straw into 3 groups and braid them. Bend the braid over to the front of the heart and wrap with wire to hold the loop. Wrap red raffia over the wire to hide it. Wrap the 2 short pieces of Scandi braid around the 2 wired sections of straw and hot-glue them in place.

Wheat Bundle

Arrange 12 wheat straws in an attractive bundle and wrap them with wire. Cover the wire with red raffia and knot. (*Note:* Soaking the straws is not necessary.)

Star

1. Soak the straw for at least 40 minutes, following the general directions on the facing page.

2. Cut an 11¼" length of floral wire and insert it into the straw. Starting with the large end of the straw, make a zigzag of bends every inch, as shown in the diagram below.

3. Pull the zigzag around so the ends touch to form a 5-pointed star. Slip the small end of the straw into the large end. Let the straw dry.

4. Decorate with a loop and tie of red raffia.

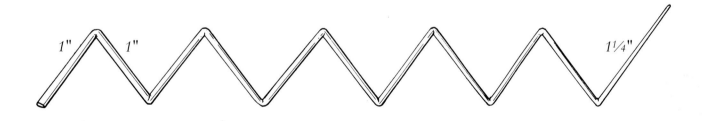

Bending Wheat for Star

Christmas Starfish Ornaments

Expressing the joy of the season, three sprightly starfish have been transformed into a Santa, a snowman, and an angel who seems to have an aura of Fairy Godmother as well. The natural shapes of the starfish exude cheerfulness, with upraised arms and dancing feet to go along with their smiling faces. In another mode altogether is the bejeweled star, which is covered with gold and glitter, fit for a king—and the top of the Christmas tree.

SIZES

Starfish ornaments shown are 5"–7" wide

NATURE'S MATERIALS

4 large starfish 5"–7" wide, with the legs all the same length, if possible

SUPPLIES AND TOOLS

Acrylic paint: white, red, peach, black, rust, blue, and gold (mix colors where necessary)

Fabric paint markers in silver glitter and gold glitter

1"-wide paintbrush

Medium paintbrush for white tacky glue

Fine paintbrush for facial details

Container of iridescent glitter

Clear acrylic spray sealer

½ yard of ⅜"-wide silver ribbon for angel

6" piece of 2"-wide white satin ribbon for angel

8" piece of 2"-wide translucent iridescent wire-edged ribbon for angel

2 silver star buttons with shanks ½" wide for angel

Toothpick for angel's wand

Flat-back gems in assorted sizes and colors for star

1 yard of gold beaded cord for star

Pieces of cord or floral wire for hangers

Wire cutters (if using wire for hangers)

Tracing paper

Scissors

White tacky glue

Hot-glue gun and glue stick

Pencil

DIRECTIONS

General

1. With the 1" paintbrush, paint the entire front and back of each starfish white. Let dry. Repeat with second coat, if necessary. Let dry.

2. With a pencil, lightly draw the details for each design onto the front of the starfish.

3. Using the photos as guides, paint each ornament according to the following instructions.

Santa

1. Paint the face and the hands peach, the boots and the belt black, the suit and the hat red. Paint the details on the face (black eyes and red mouth). Paint a gold buckle on the belt. Let dry.

2. Spray with acrylic sealer and let dry.

3. To make a hanger, hot-glue a loop of cord or floral wire onto the back of the ornament.

Angel

1. Paint the face, arms, and feet peach, leaving the legs, bodice, and hat white. Paint the hair rust. Paint the details of the face (black eyes, red mouth, and pink cheeks). Let dry thoroughly.

2. Spray with acrylic sealer and let dry.

3. Outline the edge of the dress bodice and the hat with the silver glitter fabric paint marker. Let dry thoroughly.

4. Using the fine paintbrush, brush white glue on the white bodice of the dress and on the hat. Sprinkle on iridescent glitter. Let dry.

5. To make the skirt, use the silver glitter fabric paint marker to outline one long edge of the 8" piece of wired translucent ribbon with a decorative border. Pull the wire along the other edge to gather. Wrap the gathered ribbon around the waist and secure it at the back of the starfish by twisting the ends of the wire together. Hot-glue the back opening of the skirt closed. Tie the piece of silver ribbon around the waist and fasten it into a bow.

6. Use the 6" length of white satin ribbon for the wings. Trace the wing pattern provided onto tracing paper and cut it out. Put the pattern on the ribbon, outline the shape, and cut out the wings. Run a thin line of white glue along the cut edges of the ribbon to prevent fraying. Outline the wings with silver glitter fabric paint marker.

7. Cut the shank from 1 star button and hot-glue it to the top of the hat. Paint the toothpick silver and, when it is dry, hot-glue the other star button onto it. Hot-glue the wand to the angel's hand.

8. To make a hanger, hot-glue a loop of cord or floral wire onto the back of the ornament.

Snowman

1. Paint the mittens red and the hat red and blue. Paint the details of the face (black eyes, pink cheeks, orange carrot nose, black dots for mouth) and 4 black dots for buttons on his suit. Paint the boots black. Let dry thoroughly.

2. Spray with clear acrylic sealer and let dry.

3. To make a hanger, hot-glue a loop of cord or floral wire onto the back of the ornament.

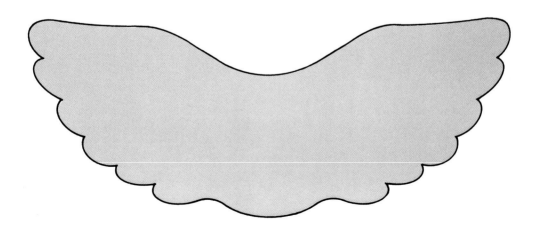

Starfish Angel Wings Pattern

Jeweled Star

1. Lightly paint the surface of the starfish with gold paint. Let dry.

2. Hot-glue gems to the starfish.

3. With gold glitter fabric paint marker, circle each gem and make squiggles all over surface of the starfish. Let dry.

4. Hot-glue gold beaded cord around the edge of the star.

5. To make a hanger, hot-glue a loop of cord or floral wire onto the back of the ornament.

Nature Crafts Basics

Throughout this book you will have encountered natural materials that have been dried, pressed, and preserved—basic techniques that are essential to making many nature craft projects. The following chapter explains these techniques, from pressing flowers to cleaning seashells, and reveals the secrets of vine wreath making, natural dyeing, and papermaking. It also describes the tools and supplies that will make the jobs easier.

You may wish to follow our project instructions step by step, or you may need some technical information before setting off on projects of your own creation. In either case, this chapter should help you with the information you need.

The resource list at the back of the book will help you locate materials not available locally.

Tools and Supplies

The few basic tools needed for nature craft projects are usually found around the house or garden shed. For the casual craftperson, scissors or a knife can substitute for pruning shears, and the simplest drill or glue gun will suffice. However, if you find yourself making more than one wreath or specializing in a particular craft, you may want to invest in better-quality tools. A good tool will make executing a project more pleasurable and will last through many future projects.

Scissors

General purpose: a lightweight 8-inch straight trimmer with comfortable plastic handles

Fabric: a straight or bent trimmer (the blade lies flat on the tabletop for cutting) made of high-carbon cutlery steel; use fabric shears only for cutting fabric

Utility Knife

General purpose: snap-off blade knife

Heavy duty: utility or mat knife with replaceable blades

Precision cutting: X-acto knife with #11 blade

Pliers

General purpose: long-nosed pliers with wire cutters

Jewelry making: flat-nosed and round-nosed pliers

Wire Cutters

General purpose: long-nosed pliers with cutter

Heavy duty: diagonal cutter; available in several sizes

Pruning Shears

General purpose: garden shears with comfortable handles and clean-cutting blades

Heavy duty: pruners with replaceable blades, wire-cutting notch, rubber-cushioned handles; available in two sizes, right- or left-handed

Loppers

General purpose: long-handled pruners for reaching higher branches and increasing leverage to cut thicker stock

Tweezers

General purpose: long, thin tweezers for handling dried flowers and leaves; helpful for hot-gluing delicate materials and gluing in narrow spaces

Drill and Drill Bits

General purpose: electric drill with interchangeable bits, including holesaws, for drilling holes ranging from 5/8" to 2" in diameter, and screwdriver bits for Phillips-head and slotted screws

Heavy duty: variable-speed, cordless, reversible driver drill for screwing as well as drilling

Glue Gun and Glue Sticks

General purpose: hot- or low-temperature glue gun, with or without trigger to feed glue stick

Heavy duty: combination 2-temperature gun with high- and low-temperature settings and combination high- and low-melt glue sticks. High-melt glue can burn fingers; low-melt glue melts at lower temperatures and, although hot, will not burn skin. High-melt glues are for bonding wood, cardboard, leather, shells; low-melt glues are for Styrofoam and other plastics and fragile dried plant materials.

Craft Glue

General purpose: white all-purpose glue for paper and dried plant materials

Heavy duty: white tacky glue for quicker adhesion; dries clear

Floral Wire

General purpose and heavy duty: flexible wire in gauges ranging from 16 (very heavy) to 30 (extremely fine); available in green or bright (shiny) finish, or with white or green cotton covering; sold in spools or cut in 12", 18", and 36" lengths

Drying Plants, Leaves, Flowers, Fruits, and Vegetables

Drying plant materials can be as simple as laying them on a radiator on a cool fall day or as scientific as a laboratory procedure. Plants, leaves, stems, seeds, and flowers can be air-dried, oven-dried, microwaved, or dried with desiccants such as cornmeal, borax, or silica gel. Sometimes flowers get dried by accident when they are put in a vase and forgotten about. The water in the plant tissue and in the vase slowly evaporates until both are bone-dry. Whichever route you choose, the element of surprise will still operate and you will need to experiment for ideal results. The more meticulous craftspeople working with an oven or microwave will take notes and record the drying times of different flowers, leaves, and stems; others will simply gather them and hang them in the barn, garage, or attic until they are dry.

In any case, for the best results, harvest the materials in dry weather before or after the heat of midday. High humidity will double the drying time and increase the chance of developing mold and mildew. Choose blossoms that have not quite reached the peak of bloom. Their petals will be less likely to drop when the flower is dried. Select healthy foliage with good color. Flowers with intense colors will retain their color better than ones with pastel shades. Save any plant material that breaks or does not dry perfectly for potpourri or papermaking.

Freeze-dried botanicals are also available through floral and craft suppliers. Freeze drying is a commercial process used primarily for larger, multipetaled flowers such as roses. It is more expensive than other drying techniques, but freeze-dried materials keep their colors longer.

AIR DRYING

1. After gathering flowers or herbs, strip off the lower leaves. If you cannot hang them for drying right away, stand them in a few inches of cold water in a cool, shady place.

2. Gather a few stalks into a loose bundle with the flower heads at different levels to encourage air circulation. Tie the base of the stems with raffia or string and hang them with their heads down from a beam or on a drying rack. A makeshift rack can be made by nailing strips of wood across the rafters in an attic. The drying area should be out of direct light with good circulation. The upper areas of buildings are dryer than basements or other spaces below grade.

3. Drying will take anywhere from a few days to several weeks, depending on the humidity. Check the bundles from time to time and tighten the ties as the plant material shrinks.

OVEN DRYING

1. Leaves, grasses, and flowers can be dried more quickly by spreading them on cookie sheets covered with paper towels and placing them in an oven set at a low temperature (about 125°–150° F). (If the oven does not maintain a low temperature, leave the door ajar to encourage air circulation.)

2. Lay a piece of wire screen over larger leaves, such as maples, which have a tendency to curl while drying. The weight of the screen alone will keep them flat.

3. Leave the material in the oven until it is crisp and dry. Some fragile leaves will take only 5–10 minutes; thicker flower heads will take longer.

DRYING WITH DESICCANTS

Sand, borax, and cornmeal are traditional desiccants (materials that absorb moisture). Today silica gel is the desiccant of choice for drying plant material, as it is much more efficient and can be used over and over again. Another advantage of silica gel is that you can tell how moist it is by its color. When damp, it is pale pink; it turns blue as it dries.

1. Dry the silica gel by placing it on a baking sheet in a warm oven. Stir it several times so it will dry evenly. Remove it from the oven and let it cool. It is best to work on a dry day so that the gel will not reabsorb moisture from the air.

2. If the silica gel is too coarse and will not sift gently between the petals of the flowers, grind it in a coffee mill or with a mortar and pestle to make it finer.

3. Prepare leaves and flowers for drying. Some flowers have stems that are too fragile to support their weight when dry. Cut the stems about 1" below the head and insert a 6" piece of floral wire up through the stem into the base of the blossom. This wire can be attached to a floral pick or a stronger dried stem or twig after the flower is dried.

4. Place about 1" of dried silica gel in the bottom of a cookie tin. Lay the flowers and leaves on top of the gel. Place fragile flower heads face down. Spoon gel around the flowers and add enough to cover the heads by at least 1". Cover the tin tightly. If the lid is not airtight, run masking tape along the seam.

5. Set the tin aside for several days. Drying time is usually about a week.

6. After you have taken out the dried botanicals, use a very small artist's paintbrush with soft bristles to brush the granules of gel from between the flower petals. Sift through the gel in the tin to remove any broken bits of leaves and stems and dry it again in the oven before storing it for future use.

MICROWAVE DRYING

Using a microwave oven speeds up the drying process. Simple, papery flowers, such as bachelor's buttons and pansies, and some delicate leafed herbs can be dried in the microwave in minutes.

1. Lay out the plants and flowers on sheets of paper towel on the microwave turntable or on a paper plate. Spread the material evenly and do not overlap.

2. Set the microwave at low power and check the material every 30 seconds for about 3 minutes. The amount of moisture in the plant material will determine the drying time.

3. Remove the material as soon as it is papery dry; do not let it go too long, as the leaves and flowers will begin to break apart.

MICROWAVE DRYING WITH DESICCANTS

Combining the microwave with desiccants is fast and produces professional-looking results. Follow the same procedure as that given for drying with desiccants, but remember that you cannot put anything metal in the microwave.

1. Cut off fragile stems about 1" below the flower heads. Do not attach metal floral wire until after the flower is removed from the microwave.

2. Place the silica gel in an open plastic or cardboard tray or box that is not held together

196

with metal staples. Lay the plant material in the gel and cover it with more gel. Set the cardboard box or tray on an open rack so the materials will dry evenly on all sides.

3. Set the microwave on low or defrost. Drying will take anywhere from 2 to 5 minutes, depending on the amount of silica gel and the moisture in the gel and plant material. You may use a nonmetal oven thermometer to monitor the temperature of the silica gel. For most plants it should read between 150° and 160° F. You may have to experiment for the best setting and length of heating. Take the tray or box out of the microwave and allow the gel to cool for several minutes before you remove the plant material.

DRYING FRUITS AND VEGETABLES

Squash, Pumpkin, and Melon Seeds

Seeds for use in embroidery (as on page 41) and other projects must be properly dried to preserve them without molding or sprouting.

1. Remove the seeds from the pulp of a melon or a squash. Place them in a strainer and swish them back and forth in a pot of sudsy water. Rinse them thoroughly.

2. Spread out the seeds on waxed paper. Dry them in a conventional or microwave oven set on low, or in a warm, dry attic. (See Oven Drying, page 195, and Microwave Drying, page 196 for details.)

3. When they are completely dried, spread the seeds on a sheet of clean paper and spray them lightly with clear acrylic sealer. Let dry. Store them in a sealed jar.

Ears of Corn

Pick ears of corn at the end of the season. Choose ears that look healthy and are free of insect damage. Peel the husks back, leaving

them attached, and hang the corn to dry. Drying will take several weeks.

Fruits

Citrus fruits—lemon, lime, orange, and grapefruit—can be air-dried on a cookie sheet placed on a radiator during fall and winter months or in the oven during the summer. Apples, pears, and other fruits with firm flesh can be air-dried on screens in an area out of direct light and with plenty of air circulation. In the winter they can be dried in a low oven, about 125°–150° F. (If the oven does not maintain a low temperature, leave the door ajar to encourage air circulation.)

Cut the fruit into slices ⅛"–¼" thick. Lay them on a cake rack and set the rack on the oven rack. Turn the fruits occasionally. Drying will take 1½ hours or more because fruits contain a lot of moisture. The fruit may not seem completely dry while still warm. Set it in a dry space with good air circulation to cool and dry further.

Gourds

Gourds are grown like squash on rambling garden vines. Their smooth skin becomes strong and hard when dry. Select gourds at the peak of growth that are free of scars or bruises. Set them in a cool, dry place out of direct light. Turn them occasionally and keep them separated so that the air can circulate around them. Over the course of several months the interior of the gourd will dry up and the outer skin will harden. You will know the gourd is dry when you can hear the seeds rattling inside. Many gourds are so hardy that they will dry naturally on the vine in the field over the winter.

Preserving Plants with Glycerin

Glycerin is a sticky, syrupy substance available at drugstores. When drawn up into the leaves and stems of plants, it preserves them and gives them a glossy finish. Its real advantage is that glycerin makes plant material much more pliable, enabling it to withstand rough handling. Oak, lemon, and bay leaves, large leaves that tend to become brittle with air drying, are good candidates for glycerin. More delicate herbs can also be preserved and will hold their scent but would, of course, no longer be edible. The color of some leaves will darken and the veins will stand out more.

1. Prepare branches of leaves by stripping off the bottom leaves, peeling back the bark, and pounding or mashing the bottom of the stems. This is to enable the glycerin solution to be absorbed easily by the plant tissue.

2. Combine 1 part glycerin to 2 parts hot water in a tall container. There should be about 2" of liquid, enough to cover the ends of the stems completely.

3. Stand the stems in the container. Set the container in a dry place out of direct light. After 2–3 days check on the plant material. If beads of glycerin have formed at the tips of the leaves, the solution has penetrated the entire plant. The beading of glycerin will be harder to detect on some plants than on others.

4. Remove the stems from the glycerin, rinse them off, and dry them. Store preserved material upright in dry containers or flat in boxes, separated by tissue or packing paper. The glycerin can be heated, strained, and stored for future use.

Pressing Flowers and Leaves

Pressing flowers is so quick and easy and yields such pleasing results that it is a wonder we do not do it more often. The big phone book method is a classic, requiring no extra equipment and hardly any thought. Merely pick a leaf or blossom, lay it flat in the middle

to back of the book, and set it aside for several weeks. Just remember to check the pages before a new phone book replaces the old one. Diarists of days past often placed blossoms of sentiment within the pages of their daily journals, giving the writings a poignant reality when read by later generations. Simple flower presses are available commercially or can be made with 2 pieces of ¼"-thick plywood, several sheets of corrugated cardboard, and 2 nylon webbing belts or 4 bolts and wing nuts to hold them together. Sheets of white blotting or watercolor paper are placed between the cardboard to absorb the moisture in the plant material. See Resources for more information.

1. Pick flowers and leaves just before their prime. Gather material when the weather is dry and before or after the heat of midday.

2. Arrange the blossoms on a sheet of blotting paper so that they do not touch. Flat flowers, such as pansies, work well, although soft-tissued flowers with rounded shapes, such as snapdragons, can also be pressed successfully. Just about any leaf, from ferns to large magnolias, can be pressed when fresh.

3. Lay a sheet of blotting paper on top of the flowers and leaves. Lay a sheet of cardboard on top of the blotting paper and sandwich everything between the wood press covers. Wrap the belts around the covers and pull them tight, or tighten the wing nuts if you are using bolts.

4. Wait several weeks for the plant material to dry completely. Handle dry material with tweezers, as it is very light and fragile.

Cleaning Shells and Other Seashore Materials

Materials that come from the sea are often saturated with salt and need rinsing in fresh water before use. Although we encourage the

gathering of empty shells, sometimes fragments of muscle cling to the shells and must
be removed. Soak shells in a mild solution of
fresh water and household bleach, rinse with
clear water, and allow to dry thoroughly
before using in a project. Starfish are best
purchased commercially. Seaweed found
dried on the beach should also be rinsed and
left out to dry before being used in a decorative project. If you are using beach sand for a
planter, rinse it with clear water and spread it
out to dry.

Basic Dyes from Plant Material

Red cabbage, onions, beets, spinach, marigolds, delphiniums, red poppies, common
plants in the vegetable and flower garden, and
more exotic plants—such as madder root,
turmeric, and logwood (not edible but very
colorful)—can all be brewed to make subtle
and unusual dyes. Almost any plant from the
garden or woods will impart some color
when steeped in boiling water. Traditional
dyes are also made from animals and minerals.
One of the strangest of these is cochineal, a
deep pink dye made from an insect that lives
on a cactus. This too is nature's product, but
one that you might prefer to purchase from
a craft supplier or yarn store that sells dyes
for yarn.

   With the exception of the more exotic
dyestuffs, infusions made from flowers and
plants create soft and subtle hues that intensify the longer you leave them in the dye bath.
Different materials will absorb dyes differently, depending on their natural color and on
how porous they are. Mordants, a medieval-
sounding ingredient, are metallic salts that
enable a material to accept the color of the
dye. For instance, wool yarn is treated with a
mordant before it is dyed. None of the projects in this book requires mordants, but you
might seek more information if you wish to
use natural dyes on other materials, fabrics, or
yarns. Infusions can also be brewed for scent,

although the aroma will also be subtle, and
not as long-lasting as that of a scented oil.

NATURE'S MATERIALS

Fresh or dried botanicals: about 1 cup of
   fresh, 2–3 tablespoons of dried

For color

Onion skins—yellow

Daffodils—bright yellow

Delphiniums—green-blue

Cochineal—dark pink

Logwood—purple, dark blue-gray

Madder root—peach

Red cabbage—light pink

For scent

Lavender

Lemon verbena

Marjoram

Mint

Rosemary

Thyme

Whole cloves

SUPPLIES AND TOOLS

1-quart bowl, heat-proof glass or stainless steel

Strainer

Measuring cup

2 cups of boiling water

DIRECTIONS

Place the botanicals in the bowl. Pour boiling
water over them. Allow the mixture to cool;
then strain out the plant material. Experiment
with quantities of plant material, length of
steeping time, and color absorption by various
products you want to dye.

   For dyeing paper pulp, see the directions in
Handmade Paper, page 204. For dyeing eggs
and eggshells, see the directions on pages 32–34.

Grapevine Wreath

A grapevine wreath is wonderfully simple to make. Take your pruning shears to an overgrown arbor or thicket and make the wreath on the spot. Midwinter is the traditional time to prune grapes to make the vines more productive, and the resulting wreath can be the base for a dried flower display to welcome spring. The same method can be used with bittersweet vine. Follow the practice of Native Americans, who harvest only small amounts from each plant, so that the plants may continue to grow and reproduce. The following directions are for any size wreath, from the tiny napkin ring shown on page 56 to the frothy gold wreath on page 177.

SIZE

Any size

NATURE'S MATERIALS

Grape or other vines

SUPPLIES AND TOOLS

Pruning shears

Floral wire (optional)

Wire cutters (optional)

DIRECTIONS

1. Cut a long vine. Take one end of it in one hand. Bend it with your other hand a few times into a circle of the size you want your wreath to be. Hold the vine at the point where it overlaps and tuck its free end into a gap between the vines. Take another length of vine, weave it in and out of the circle, and tuck its end in as before. If the vines are not fresh or are too stiff to bend into the tight curves of smaller wreaths, wrap them in a loose circle and soak them in a bucket of water until they become more pliable.

2. Fill in with more vines until the wreath is thick and full-looking. Wedge the ends of the vines in between the strands of the wreath as you go along. Look for thinner strands of vine with curly tendrils or leaves to make the wreath more interesting. The shape need not be perfectly round or uniform; the charm of vine wreaths lies in their rusticity, peeling bark, and wiggly strands.

Handmade Paper

Papermaking by the following technique benefits nature by recycling paper already in our homes instead of using nature's materials—trees, flax, and cotton rag—directly. Paper is made by chopping cellulose (wood, rags, or used paper) into a pulp, soaking it, and then spreading the pulp out flat to dry. Old telephone books with pastel pages, colored tissue paper, and egg cartons all work well and will impart their tint to the paper. Any paper without a glossy surface, such as copy paper, packing paper, brown paper grocery bags, or newsprint, can be recycled. You can even add the fluff from the dryer, which will contribute color and texture. Paper printed with ink will add gray tones. Newspaper is not recommended; its acid content will shorten the life of the paper. Watercolor paper, or any paper with a high cotton or linen rag content, will result in pulp that will hold together better. Try to include some paper with rag content.

The fun part of papermaking lies in the color, texture, and scent you can give your paper by using sprigs, leaves, and petals of flowers and herbs (dried or pressed), as well as colorful fibers, bits of thread, and raffia. The paper pulp can also be dyed and scented with natural infusions brewed from flowers, leaves, and bark. See Basic Dyes from Plant Materials, page 199 for lists of suggested plant materials. For photographs and examples of handmade paper projects, see pages 46 and 163.

Before we begin the instructions for papermaking, a few technical words may need explanation:

Mold and **deckle:** The mold is a simple frame with nylon mesh stretched across it that holds the pulp while it settles and dries to become paper. It can be a painting stretcher or a picture frame. The deckle is a frame that fits on top of the mold. Its center is left open and its sides determine the size of the finished piece of paper.

Couching cloth: This is the cloth the wet paper pulp lies on as the water drains from it. The couching cloth is spread over a mound of newspapers (**couching mound**), which acts as an elevated surface from which the water drains and into which it is absorbed.

Pulling: The action of moving the mold and deckle to the bottom of the container holding the pulp and water mixture, skimming the bottom, and raising the mold and deckle up through the mixture so that the pulp coats the nylon mesh, thereby allowing a sheet of paper to form.

Papermaking equipment and materials are available by mail (see Resources).

NATURE'S MATERIALS

Dried and/or pressed leaves and flowers, potpourri, herbs, raffia, etc., for added texture and color

Plant materials for dyeing and/or scenting paper pulp, if desired: about 1 cup of fresh, 2–3 tablespoons of dried leaves, petals, and stems (see Basic Dyes from Plant Material, page 199)

SUPPLIES AND TOOLS

Threads, floss, dryer fluff, silk fabric shreds, etc., for added texture and color

Used paper

Blender

Two 8" × 10" pieces of smooth-surfaced hardboard or acrylic for pressing boards

Two 8" × 10" stretcher frames or picture frames for mold and deckle

Nylon mesh or netting (about 50 holes to an inch) to stretch over a frame

Dishpan

Shallow oblong tray, large roasting pan, or kitty litter pan, large enough to hold pressing board

Smooth kitchen cloths for couching cloths

Staple gun

Iron

Pitcher for water

Newspaper

To Dye or Scent Paper (optional)

1-quart bowl, heat-proof glass or stainless steel

1-quart jar for each infusion

Strainer

Measuring cup

2 cups of boiling water

DIRECTIONS

To Make the Mold and Couching Mound

1. Make the mold by wetting the nylon mesh, stretching it tight over one of the frames, and stapling it along the outside edge of the frame. (The deckle is the other frame, which fits over the mold.)

2. Make the couching mound by laying one of the pressing boards in the shallow tray. Fold 3 sheets of newspaper into 3 different-sized pieces: small, medium, and large. Place the small piece on the pressing board first; layer on the medium and then the large wad. Pour about a cup of water over the pieces until they form a mound. Next, cover the mound with a damp couching cloth.

To Make the Pulp

1. Tear the paper into pieces about 1" square. Fill the blender about ⅔ full with the torn pieces and add water to the height of the paper. Blend on high speed for 30 seconds. To

avoid damaging the motor, don't blend for more than 10 seconds without stopping for a moment. The paper should liquefy and the mixture should take on a milky appearance. To make 10 sheets of paper, you will have to repeat this step 5 more times.

2. Add clean water to the dishpan until it is ½ full.

3. Pour the pulp into the dishpan of water. Continue to blend until all the paper is pulped and added to the dishpan. As you are pulping the paper in the blender, stir the mixture in the dishpan frequently to prevent the fibers from settling to the bottom.

4. If you want to color the paper or add a scent, see the instructions on page 204 for making infusions.

5. If you are adding potpourri, dried leaves or flowers, pressed flowers, or any other decorative materials to the paper, put them into the pulp mixture now. They will become part of the paper when you pull it.

To Pull a Piece of Paper

1. To pull a sheet of paper, place the deckle on top of the mold with the mesh side up. Holding the deckle and the mold together at the sides, slip them into the pulp/water mixture at about a 45° angle (diagram A), skimming the bottom of the dishpan, and move them into a flat position. Then bring the mold and deckle straight up, catching an even coating of pulp on the mesh and lifting it up out of the pan (diagram B). The water will drain through the mesh. (If the mesh is not entirely covered with pulp, reimmerse the frames into the pulp/water mixture.) Gently shake the mold to help the fibers settle. As the pulp becomes more solid, hold the frames steady, so that the sheet forms. If you have added pressed leaves, petals, and so on to the pulp mixture, press them gently into the drying pulp.

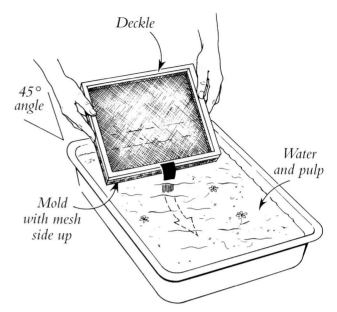

A. *Slip mold and deckle into pulp and water at approximately a 45° angle*

2. When the water has stopped draining, lift off the deckle. Check to see that the couching cloth you placed over the mound is still damp and wrinkle-free. (Wrinkles will leave impressions on the finished paper.) Place the mold in the shallow tray. With the mold on the edge

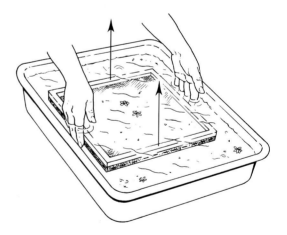

B. *Submerge mold and deckle, level off, and lift straight up*

of the couching cloth and the pulp toward the couching mound, flip the mold over so that the pulp is deposited on the mound (diagrams C1, C2, and C3). This is much like flipping a cake pan over a plate. Don't try to move the pulp; if you do, it will tear or crumble. If the pulp sticks to the mold, remove the pulp from

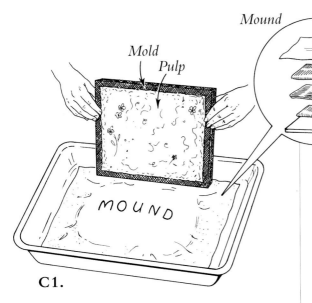

Mound

Mold

Pulp

Cloth

Folded sheets of newspaper

Pressing board

M O U N D

C1.

the mold, return the mold to the dishpan, and start again. Use a clean couching cloth and remoisten the mound before pulling another sheet of paper.

C2. *Roll pulp firmly over mound*

3. To make the second sheet of paper, lay another damp couching cloth over the sheet of pulp, being sure to smooth it out. Repeat these steps, continuing to layer sheets of pulp

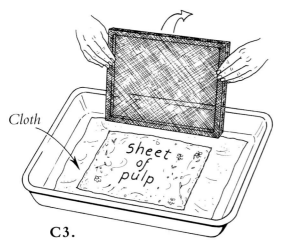

Cloth

sheet of pulp

C3.

and damp couching cloths. If the pulp/water mixture becomes too thin, add more pulp to the dishpan. Add more dried or pressed botanicals or other materials to the top of the pulp/water mixture to vary the textures of the paper as you work.

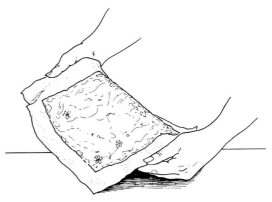

D. *Wet pulp holding its shape on cloth*

4. After you have finished the layers, put a damp couching cloth over the last sheet; then put the second pressing board on top of the layered sheets. About 10 sheets of paper can be pressed at the same time. Holding all the layers together between the pressing boards, flip the whole stack over. Lift the pressing board that had previously been on the bottom and remove the couching mound. In its place put a folded sheet of dry newspaper. Replace the pressing board, flip the stack over, and squeeze the boards together, extracting as much water as you can. Most of the excess water will be absorbed by the newspaper.

5. Remove the top pressing board and the first cloth. Then carefully lift off each couching cloth and its sheet of pulp (diagram D). Leave the sheets on their cloths and place them on sheets of newspaper to dry. This may take as long as a day.

6. The couching cloths will give the paper a textured surface. If you prefer a smoother finish, iron the paper while it is still damp on the couching cloth or transfer it to a smooth surface (the pressing board or a nonstick cookie sheet) and iron it with a low setting.

7. Gently peel the paper away from the cloth or ironing surface, starting at one corner.

To Color Pulp with Natural Infusions

1. In a heat-proof bowl place 1 cup of fresh plant material or 2–3 tablespoons of dried material. Add 2 cups of boiling water. Allow to cool. Leave until the infusion is very strong. For certain vegetable infusions, such as onion skins, simmer for 30–60 minutes. Experiment with plant infusions before you begin the papermaking project, and remember that the content of the pulp will affect how it absorbs color.

2. Scoop up about 2 cups of pulp from the dishpan mixture, strain out the water into the dishpan, and transfer the pulp to a quart jar. When the infusion is strong enough, strain out the plant material and transfer the liquid to the quart jar with the pulp. Leave the pulp in the jar with the dye for an hour or two, or until it has absorbed the desired amount of color. The pulp will dry lighter.

3. Pour the pulp back into the dishpan and proceed with step 1 for pulling paper.

To Scent Pulp with Natural Infusions

Follow the method just described for coloring pulp. Strain out the plant material and add the infusion to the dishpan of pulp/water mixture. This liquid should be counted as 2 cups of the total liquid in the dishpan.

Resources

ADHESIVES

Activa Products, Inc.
700 South Garrett
P.O. Box 1296
Marshall, TX 75671

For Mighty Tacky™ craft glue.

Black & Decker, Inc.
1061 Old Country Road
Westbury, NY 11590

Two-temperature and low-temperature glue guns.
Available at hardware, variety, and craft supply stores.

BEADS

The Beadery
P.O. Box 178
105 Canonchet Road
Hope Valley, RI 02832

Manufacturer of beads, beading supplies. Catalog.

CANDY MOLDS

Wilton Enterprises, Inc.
2240 West 75th Street
Woodridge, IL 60517

For heart-shaped candy molds.

DRIED AND PRESSED PLANT MATERIALS

American Oak Preserving Company, Inc.
P.O. Box 187
North Judson, IN 46366

Raffia in colors, preserved oak leaves. Write for
information and list of retail sources.

Mills Floral Company
4550 Peachtree Lakes Drive
Duluth, GA 30136

For dried citrus fruits, apples, flowers, foliage,
wreath forms. For brochure send SASE.

Sunny Acres Wheat
P.O. Box 218
Howard, KS 67349

For dried wheat, flowers, herbs, and spices.
For catalog send SASE.

EVERGREENS AND WREATHS

All Western Evergreen Nursery
6840 Liberty Pole Road
Webster's Crossing, NY 14584

Country Christmas Shoppe
10260 Pennycook Road
Hunt, NY 14846

For fresh wreaths of Douglas fir, spruce, and
Concolor, a nonallergenic, soft blue-green evergreen
that holds up well in hot weather and is ideal for
holiday decorations in warm climates.

Members of the New York
Christmas Tree Growers Association, Inc.
646 Finches Corner Road
Red Creek, NY 13143

FABRICS

Blueprints-Printables
1504 Industrial Way, #7
Belmont, CA 94002

For 8" squares of pretreated cotton for sunprinting.

FEATHERS

Zucker Feather Products
P.O. Box 331
512 North East Street
California, MO 65018

For packaged feathers and plastic mask forms.

GARDEN TOOLS

Smith & Hawkin
P.O. 6907
Florence, KY 41022-6907

For pruning shears, loppers, flower press, and blotting paper.

LEATHER AND SINEW

Eagle Feather Trading Post
168 West 12th Street
Ogden, UT 84404

Catalog $3.

Van Dyke's Restorers
P.O. Box 278
Woonsocket, SD 57385

For leather lacing, craft tools. Catalog.

PAINT

Chase Products
P.O. Box 70
Maywood, IL 60153

For Champion Sprayon™ gold and silver spray.

Modern Options
2325 Third Street, #339
San Francisco, CA 94107

For Copper Topper, Patina Green, Patina Antiquing Kit.

Plaid Enterprises, Inc.
P.O. Box 7600
Norcross, GA 30091

For Mod-Podge™ acrylic varnish, adhesive, and sealer; in matte and gloss finishes.

PAPERMAKING SUPPLIES

Carriage House Paper
79 Guernsey Street
Brooklyn, NY 11222

For papermaking kits, molds and deckles, screening. Catalog.

RIBBONS

CM Offray & Sons
Route 24
Chester, NJ 07930

Write for list of retail suppliers.

SEEDS

The Cook's Garden
P.O. Box 535
Londonderry, VT 05148

For ornamental corn and vegetable seeds. Catalog $1.

SELF-HARDENING CLAY

American Art Clay Co., Inc.
4717 West 16th Street
Indianapolis, IN 46222

For Mexican Pottery Clay, rust-red; and Marblex clay, gray.

WOOD PRODUCTS

Shaker Workshops
P.O. Box 1028
Concord, MA 01742-1028

For painted wood trays, hand mirrors. Catalog.

Sudberry House
Box 895
Old Lyme, CT 06371

For box used in Seed Embroidery project. Catalog.

Unfinished Business, Inc.
P.O. Box 246
Wingate, NC 28174

For unfinished wood trays, boxes, birdhouses. Catalog.

Index

Page numbers in bold indicate photos.

Bamboo:
    Easels, 99-100, **101**
    Walking Stick, 104, **105**
Bark:
    Berry Basket, 57, **58**
    Birch, Box, 67, **68**
    Birch, Ornaments, **68,** 69
    Birch, Wreath, **68,** 69
    Wall Pocket, **58,** 59
Basket(s):
    Bark Berry, 57, **58**
    Bittersweet, 88, **89**
    Crocheted Raffia, 96, **97,** 98
    Twig Easter, 168, **169**
Bead jewelry, 110, **111,** 112-13
Birdbath, Branch, 64, **65,** 66
Birdhouses:
    Gourd, 24, **25**
    Seed-Covered, 37-38, **39,** 40
Boats, Twig, 106, **107**
Box(es):
    Birch Bark, 67, **68**
    Handmade Gift, 45, **46,** 47
    Scallop Shell, 132, **133**
    Shell-Covered, 134, **135**
Branch:
    Birdbath, 64, **65,** 66
    Table Lamp, 60, **61,** 62

Candles:
    Pressed-Flower, 28, **29**
    Twig Torchères, **61,** 63
Centerpiece:
    Cornucopia, 173, **174**
    Pumpkin, **179,** 179-80
Christmas Ornaments, Starfish, 188,
    189, 190-91, **191;** *see also*
        Ornaments
Clay Bead Jewelry, 110, **111,**
    112-13
Corn:
    Drying ears of, 197
    Ornamental, 183, **183**
Cornucopia Centerpiece, 173, **174**
Crocheted Raffia Baskets, 96, **97,**
    98
Crystal Jewelry, **127,** 128

Curtain:
    Holdback, Shell, **147,** 148
    Pole Finial, Starfish, 152, **153**
    Ring Covers, Shell-and Starfish,
        149, **150,** 151
    Tieback, Raffia-and-Shell, 146,
        147

Découpage:
    Pressed-Flower Lampshade, 18,
        19
Dolls, Spring and Fall, **73,** 78-81
Dresser Set, Shell, 136, **137**
Driftwood-and-Sand Frame, 117,
    118
Drying plant materials, 195-97
Dyes and dying, 199

Easels, Bamboo, 99-100, **101**
Easter:
    Basket, Twig, 168, **169**
    Egg Bunny, **169,** 170
Egg(s):
    Easter, Bunny, **169,** 170
    Leaf-Resist, Dyed, and Gilded,
        169, 171-72
    Patinated, 166-67, **167**
Eggshell:
    Mosaic Frame, 32, **33,** 34
    Vases, **33,** 34
Embroidery, Seed, 41-42, **43,** 44

Fabrics, seasonal, 81
Ferns, Pressed, 120, **121**
Finials:
    Curtain Pole, Starfish, 152, **153**
    Lamp, Shell, 140, **141**
Flowerpot, Moss-Covered, 114,
    115
Flowers:
    Door Spray, 102, **103**
    Drying of, 195-97
    Floral Picture Frame, **13,** 14
    Language of, 12
    Lavender Sachets, **21,** 22-23
    Pressed-, Candles and Floral
        Candle Wreath, 28, **29**

Pressed-, Lampshade, 18, **19**
Pressing, 198
Preserving, 197-98
Teacup Tussie-mussie, 12, **13**
-Trimmed Hat, **21,** 23
Valentines, Handmade, 162, **163**
Flower Vase, Pinecone, **174,** 175
Frame:
    Driftwood-and-Sand, 117, **118**
    Eggshell Mosaic, 32, **33,** 34
    Floral Picture, **13,** 14
Fruit:
    Citrus Box and Pouch, **35,** 36
    Dried Citrus Wreath, 26, **27**
    Drying, 36, 195-97
Furniture, Miniature Twig, 72, **73,**
    74-77

Garland:
    Bittersweet Door, 86, **87**
    Gilded Magnolia, and Spray,
        156, **157,** 158-59
    Mantel, **181,** 181-82
Gift:
    Box, Handmade, 45, **46,** 47
    Wrap, Gilded, **157,** 160, **161**
Glycerin, preserving with, 197-98
Gourd(s):
    Birdhouse, 24, **25**
    Drying, 197
Grass, Wild, Sheaf, 84, **85**

Hat, Flower-Trimmed, **21,** 23
Herb(s):
    Kitchen Topiary, 30, **31**
    Wreath, 20, **21**
Holdback, Shell Curtain, **147,** 148
Hold-downs, Tablecloth, 144, **145**

Jewelry:
    Clay Bead, 110, **111,** 112-13
    Crystal, 127, **128**

Lamp:
    Finials, Shell, 140, **141**
    Table, Branch, 60, **61,** 62

Lampshade, Pressed-Flower, 18, **19**
Leaves:
    Gilded Gift Wrap, **157,** 160, **161**
    Gilded Magnolia Garland and
        Sprays, 156, **157**
    Maple Leaf Roses, 50, **51**
    Oak Leaf Wreath, 52, **53**
    Pressing, 198
    Stenciled Leaf Napkin and
        Gilded Acorn Napkin Ring,
        53, 55, 56
    Stenciled Leaf Tray, **53,** 54-55

Masks:
    Displaying, 95
    Feather, 93, **94,** 95
    Wood Nymph, 70, **71**
Moss:
    -Covered Flowerpot, 114, **115**
    Wreath, **115,** 116

Napkin:
    Ring, Gilded Acorn, **53, 55, 56**
    Stenciled Leaf, **53, 55, 56**
Note Paper, Handmade, 45, **46**

Ornaments:
    Birch Bark, **68,** 69
    Braided-Wheat, 184, **185,** 186-87
    Christmas Starfish, 188, **189,**
        190-91, **191**
    Patinated Eggs, 166-67, **167**

Paper, Handmade:
    Handmade Note Paper, Gift
        Boxes, and Bookmark, 45, **46,** 47
    Valentines, 162, **163**
Papermaking, 200-204
Pinecone Flower Vase, **174,** 175
Planter, Twig, **91,** 92
Preserving plants with glycerin,
    197-98
Pressing flowers and leaves, 198
Pumpkin Centerpiece, **179,** 179-80

Sachets:
    Lavender, **21,** 22-23
    Sunprint, 124, **125,** 126

Sand:
    Driftwood-and-, Frame, 117,
        118
    Southwest, Garden, **118,** 119
Seed(s):
    Drying, 197
    Embroidery, 41-42, **43,** 44
Sewing:
    Lavender Sachets, **21,** 22-23
    Spring and Fall Dolls, **73,** 78-81
    Sunprint Sachets, 124, **125,** 126
Shell(s):
    -and-Starfish Curtain Ring
        Covers, 149, **150,** 151
    Cleaning, 198-99
    -Covered Box, 134, **135**
    Dresser Set, 136, **137**
    Holdback, Curtain, **147,** 148
    Hold-downs, Tablecloth, 144,
        145
    Lamp Finials, 140, **141**
    Scallop, Boxes, 132, **133**
    Tieback, Raffia and, 146, **147**
    Topiaries, Seashell, 142, **143**
    Wreath, 138, **139**
Spray(s):
    Door, 102, **103**
    Gilded Magnolia Garland and,
        156, **157,** 158-59
Stenciled:
    Leaf Napkin and Gilded Acorn
        Napkin Ring, **53, 55, 56**
    Leaf Tray, **53,** 54-55
Stones:
    Herb Markers, 122, **123**
    Wire-wrapping, 127
Sunprint Sachets, 124, **125,** 126

Tablecloth Hold-downs, 144, **145**
Table Lamp, Branch, 60, **61,** 62
Techniques:
    Cleaning of seashore materials,
198-99
    Drying plant materials, 195-97
    Dyes and dying, 199
    Papermaking, 200-204
    Preserving plants, 197-98
    Pressing flowers and leaves, 198

Tieback, Raffia-and-Shell, 146, **147**
Tools and Supplies, 194-95
Topiary:
    Ivy, Wreaths and Tree, 15, **16,**
        17
    Kitchen, 30, **31**
    Seashell, 142, **143**
    Spiral, 176, **177,** 178
Torchères, Twig, **61,** 63
Tray, Stenciled Leaf, **53,** 54, 55
Tussie-mussies, Teacup, 12, **13**
Twig:
    Boats, 106, **107**
    Easter Basket, 168, **169**
    Furniture, Miniature, 72, **73,**
        74-77
    Planter, **91,** 92
    Swirl Wreath, 90, **91**
    Torchères, **61,** 63

Valentines, Handmade, 162, **163**
Vase(s):
    Eggshell, **33,** 34
    Flower, Pinecone, **174,** 175
Vine(s):
    Bittersweet Basket, 88, **89**
    Bittersweet Door Garland, 86,
        87
    Golden Grapevine Wreath, **177,**
        178
    Grapevine Wreath, 200
    Patinated Wreath, 164, **165**

Walking Sticks, 104, **105**
Wall Pocket, Bark, 58, **59**
Wreath:
    Birch Bark, **68,** 69
    Dried Citrus, 26, **27**
    Floral Candle, 28, **29**
    Golden Grapevine, **177,** 178
    Grapevine, 200
    Herb, 20, **21**
    Ivy Topiary, and Tree, 15, **16,** 17
    Moss, **115,** 116
    Oak Leaf, 52, **53**
    Patinated, 164, **165**
    Shell, 138, **139**
    Twig Swirl, 90, **91**